Words across the Taiwan Strait

A Critique of Beijing's "White Paper" on China's Reunification

John F. Copper

University Press of America, Inc.
Lanham • New York • London

University Press of America,® Inc.
4720 Boston Way
Lanham, Maryland 20706

3 Henrietta Street
London, WC2E 8LU England

Copublished by arrangement with
the East Asia Research Institute.

Library of Congress Cataloging-in-Publication Data

Copper, John Franklin.
Words across the Taiwan Strait : a critique of Beijing's "White Paper"
on China's reunification / by John F. Copper.
p. cm.
Includes bibliographical references.
1. China—Politics and government—1976- 2. Taiwan—Politics and
government—1988-. 3. Chinese reunification question, 1949- I. Title.
DS779.26.C67   1995   95-6830
327.5105124'9—dc20   CIP

ISBN 0-8191-9908-7 (cloth: alk: paper)
ISBN 0-8191-9909-5 (pbk: alk: paper)

Table of Contents

Preface

The year 1989 was a watershed year. It marked the beginning of the end of the Soviet bloc and communism in the West. It witnessed the start of the demise of bipolarity and the appearance of what many described as a new world order. These events spelled the end of what some called the "China card"--or a crucial role accorded the People's Republic of China (PRC) by the United States and other world powers to offset or balance the threat of Soviet hegemony.

This same year saw the People's Liberation Army use machine guns and tanks against democracy movement supporters in Beijing--in what became known as the Tiananmen Massacre. The People's Republic of China was condemned and retreated into isolation as a result.

Across the Taiwan Strait, meanwhile, in 1987, martial law was terminated in the Republic of China (ROC). Soon after the government allowed its citizens to take trips across the Strait. Trade and investments flourished. In 1989, just a few months after the massacre in Tiananmen Square, there was a national election on the other side of the Strait. The opposition party, the Democratic Progressive Party (DPP), made impressive gains at the polls, prompting most observers to say that the ROC now had a two-party system and democracy. At this time, one pundit reported that "Taiwan had shed its pariah image and had passed it over to Beijing."

If not everyone was convinced that Taiwan was a democracy, they were in 1991 when the "elder parliamentarians" resigned from the ROC's elected bodies of government and a plenary election was held for the National Assembly. Also, if the ruling Nationalist Party or Kuomintang (KMT) had not earlier had a mandate from the people to rule Taiwan, it did now. It won the election by a big margin on a "level playing field." Meanwhile, President Lee Teng-hui ended the state of war that existed with the PRC and the "Temporary Provisions" that had circumvented some provisions of the Constitution and, thus, put into full force the promises of civil and political liberties in the that document.

The following year, in 1992, another election was held--to the legislative branch of government, or the Legislative Yuan. This time the DPP had learned a lesson: that making Taiwan independence an issue, which it had done by putting it in its platform during the campaign for the 1991 election, was counterproductive. But, it had learned more than this; it also learned what issues were important to the electorate and how better to present its views. It thus performed well in the 1992 election. So well that some of its leaders speculated that the opposition party would control the government in a few years. If that was an exaggeration most observers took the DPP seriously after this election "victory." However, others said that the KMT had already weathered the storm caused by a new and different world order, or "disorder," that evicted ruling parties throughout the world. Good performances in subsequent local elections provided some evidence that this was the case.

Of greater relevance to the issue to be discussed here, during its various election campaigns the DPP had made the case that the ROC was isolated and in danger of being rendered illegitimate by Beijing's diplomatic efforts to isolate Taipei. It called for participation in the United Nations. The KMT could not disagree. Moreover, Germany had become unified after cross recognition and joint or dual membership in the United Nations. "Why not the two Chinas?" some asked. Taipei was also in possession of an enviable foreign exchange position at a time when economic power seemed to have replaced military power in the new world order equation. And its diplomatic position was stronger due to democratization on its side of the Taiwan Strait and human rights abuses, which were now being noticed, on the other.

It was in that context that Taipei took the offensive to improve its diplomatic ties and its status in the international community. Beijing responded with stepped up efforts to isolate the ROC. It also bolstered its military with new weapons' acquisitions that had application in the Taiwan Strait--to intimidate Taipei. The United States and France responded in 1992 with new arms sales to the Taiwan.

In was then that Beijing published its "White Paper." Similarly, and in this milieu and in response to Beijing's publication of the document in question, the Mainland Affairs Council in Taipei published a response a few months later.

In the pages that follow the reader will find the author's analysis and critique of the "White Paper." Following, in Appendix I, is the said document. Appendix II is Taipei's response issued in July 1994 entitled "Relations Across the Taiwan Strait." In that "report" the ROC stated its position, calling for "two equal political entities"--as opposed to Beijing's "one country, two systems." The media in Beijing responded that this document presented a distorted picture of the Taiwan question, constituted advocating two Chinas and "would be refuted in due course." Also, in Appendix III, the reader will find the ROC's "Guidelines for National Unification," passed into law in early 1991. Some observers have stated the opinion that Beijing should have replied to this earlier document, but did not.

John F. Copper
November 1994

A Critique of Beijing's "White Paper"

I

In August 1993, the Taiwan Affairs Office and Information Office of the State Council of the People's Republic of China published a document called "The Taiwan Question and the Reunification of China."[1] (See Appendix I.)   This 24-page pamphlet, or booklet, subsequently became known as Beijing's "White Paper" on Taiwan. Both the timing of the publication and its contents appear to reflect opposition by the government of the People's Republic of China to the Republic of China making a bid to participate in the United Nations and/or other international governmental organizations and probably concern over the ROC's recent active and successful diplomacy aimed at greater participation in international politics.[2]

The ROC's President Lee Teng-hui a few months earlier declared that Taiwan would seek to participate in the United Nations, after which the Ministry of Foreign Affairs in Taipei adopted measures to translate this into a specific policy and implemented that policy.[3] Several other government agencies and the ruling Nationalist Party, supported by the opposition Democratic Progressive Party, lent strong support.   In August, just at the time the "White Paper" was published, seven Central American countries sent a jointly-signed letter to U.N. Secretary-General Boutros Boutros-Ghali requesting that the United Nations consider parallel representation in the world body for Taipei and Beijing--a move that was signaled in advance and could have been anticipated several months before it happened. At this time a number of newspapers around the world carried articles supporting the ROC

---

1. Beijing: Taiwan Affairs Office and Information Office, State Council, 1993.

2. The United Nations General Assembly was scheduled to open less than a month later, on September 21. One of the issues that was going to be discussed was the ROC's participation as proposed by seven Central American nations.

3. President Lee made this statement in April. It is also noteworthy that the Legislative Yuan had passed a bill calling for Taiwan to push for membership in the U.N. in 1991.

bid, or at least suggesting that Taiwan should not be isolated from the world community.

The "White Paper" was published in a number of foreign languages, even Korean (which was unusual considering the fact that few such documents have been published in Korean). A large number of copies were printed. Most observers considered the document to represent the PRC's official line on the status of Taiwan. According to one observer, it was the work of Taiwan specialists at the Chinese Academy of Social Sciences, the Ministry of Foreign Affairs and a task force headed by President and Chinese Communist Party General Secretary Jiang Zemin.[4] Most also regarded it as an effort to refute the argument that the ROC is a legally constituted nation-state and deserves to play a role in governmental international organizations. Similarly, the PRC seemed to respond to actions by advocates of Taiwan separation or independence; thus they argued that any other national title that might replace the Republic of China or any independence effort is not legitimate.[5]

---

4. Julian Baum, "Divided Nations," *Far Eastern Economic Review*, September 16, 1993, p. 10.

5. It is worth noting that independence advocates, particularly the Democratic Progressive Party, which registered a major victory in the 1992 election, had suggested that the ROC change its name to "Republic of Taiwan" in order to bolster the nation's claim to sovereignty in view of Taipei's foreign policy and diplomatic setbacks. In fact, it made this charge beginning in the 1970s (as *tangwai*, before it was a political party) and in the 1991 election. For details, see John F. Copper, *Taiwan's 1991 and 1992 Non-Supplemental Elections: Reaching a Higher State of Democracy* (Lanham, MD: University Press of America, 1994), p. 8, p. 30 and p. 54.

That leaders in Beijing were sensitive to this also seems clear. Three months after the DPP "victory" in the 1992 election, Premier Li Peng declared that the People's Republic of China "will take all necessary *drastic* [italics added] measures to stop any activities aimed at making Taiwan independent and splitting the motherland." These remarks appeared in *People's Daily*, March 16, 1993.

Still others have said that Beijing was troubled by a combination of Taiwan's economic clout in a new international order that was built on economic relations, plus the 1992 election. See, for example, Yu-shan Wu, "Taiwan in 1993: Attempting a Diplomatic Breakthrough," *Asian Survey*, January 1994, p. 52.

The document in question is divided into a foreword, conclusion and five substantive chapters. The five main chapters are entitled: 1. Taiwan--an Inalienable Part of China, 2. Origin of the Taiwan Question, 3. The Chinese Government's Basic Position Regarding Settlement of the Taiwan Question, 4. Relations Across Taiwan Straits: Evolution and Stumbling Blocks, 5. Several Questions Involving Taiwan in International Relations.

Below the author will critique the arguments and positions enunciated in the various segments of this document. In so doing, the PRC's policy and its views on the issue of Taiwan's status will hopefully be clarified to some degree. The writer expects also to shed some light on the future of relations between Beijing and Taipei.

II

In the first chapter of this document, the authors present the argument that Taiwan is geologically and historically a part of China. It begins: "Lying off the ... coast of the China mainland, Taiwan ... forms an integral whole with the mainland." At first blush this statement seems axiomatic or a point not worth arguing. Yet it has been challenged by geological evidence that Taiwan has another origin-- the same as others in the chain of volcanic islands extending from the Alaska Aleutians to Japan south to the Ryukyu Islands and to Taiwan and on to the Philippines and southward.[6] In any event, it is clearly not credible to say with certitude that Taiwan "forms an integral whole with the mainland." ROC scholars have discussed this issue and feel that Taiwan's geological origins are not the same as the Ryukyu Islands or the Philippines and that Taiwan indeed was once part of the Asian mainland; however, they also say this issue is subject to speculation and needs further research.[7]

---

6. W.G. Goddard, *Formosa: A Study in Chinese History* (East Lansing, MI: Michigan State University Press, 1966), pp. x-xi.

7. It should be noted in this connection that while China is an advanced nation in many fields of science, geology and anthropology are not among them.

ROC scholars have also noted that differences in geological origins, which is indicated by variances between soil, plant and animal life, etc. between Taiwan and the mainland is not a very significant point since such differences--in fact, greater differences--exist between north and south or east and west in China.

The argument then proceeds citing "factual evidence" of China's historical contacts with Taiwan--without mentioning the original inhabitants of the island. According to most experts, humans inhabited Taiwan probably more than ten thousand years ago. Their descendants are currently known as the *yuan chu min* (original people) or Aborigines.[8] Their origins are uncertain; but linguistic similarities with the people of present day Malaysia and Indonesia suggest they came from Southeast Asia. Other studies indicate they may have come from south China. Still another explanation is that they have several origins, including possibly Japan and North China.[9] In any event, by omitting any discussion of the original inhabitants of Taiwan, who incidently lay claim to the island, the document seems *prima facia* to use information about Taiwan's history selectively and without regard to important facts--in this case, who inhabited the island first and whether their descendants have a legal claim to Taiwan.[10]

They also point out that geological evidence such as the curvature of Taiwan's mountain ranges and the strait shores on Taiwan as well as the adjacent coast of China, suggest to Taiwan broke off from China at some time in the past. The depth of the Taiwan Strait and the age of rock formations in Taiwan strongly indicate that its origins are not the same as the Ryukyu Islands or the Philippines. For details, see Chiao-min Hsieh, *Taiwan: Ilha Formosa: A Geographical Perspective* (Washington, DC: Butterworths, 1964), pp. 2-4.

8. They are referred to in the ROC's Constitution as *Shan pao* or mountain compatriots. In 1992, aboriginal leaders sought to have this term changed to *yuan chu min*, which is probably best translated "original inhabitants." Some scholars objected to this term--saying that archaeological evidence suggests even earlier inhabitants of the island. See *Republic of China Yearbook 1994* (Taipei: Government Information Office, 1994) p. 35.

9. James W. Davidson, *The Island of Formosa: Past and Present* (New York: Oxford University Press, 1988) p. 3. Still other origins have been suggested. According to another author, recent archaeological evidence, based on the burial practices of the earliest human inhabitants of Taiwan, indicates similarities with both the Philippines and India. Also, see Chen Wen-tsung, "Building on the Past," *Free China Review*, June 1992, p. 85.

10. While the Aborigines of Taiwan make up only a very small percent of the population of the island (less than 2 percent) and such ancient claims of ownership are not regarded highly in international law, such groups are having

To be convincing the authors should have noted that the Aboriginal languages are Sinitic or Chinese in origin (as are all of the languages of Southeast Asia) and that proximity indicates that Taiwan's geological and historical ties are obviously closer to China than any other nation or civilization of East Asia.[11] They might also have noted that myths about the origins of the island and its people link it to China.[12]

The historical argument is fraught with still other problems. It begins with the names given to Taiwan in antiquity, one of them being Liuqiu (or Liu Chiu)--the Chinese term for the Japanese Ryukyu Islands to the north of Taiwan. The lack of consistency of names together with the spotty records in Chinese history has led Western historians to doubt information about Taiwan in early Chinese records. Clearly ROC scholars have made a better argument regarding historical ties between Taiwan and China. As one author notes, the *Shang Shu*, written 4,000 years ago, contains a geographic survey that divides China into different parts, one of which seems to include Taiwan.[13] Clearly this constitutes less problematic evidence that Taiwan has ancient ties with the mainland and certainly cannot be refuted.

Next, the argument is made that expeditions "numbering over ten thousand men" were sent to Taiwan by the State of Wu (third century A.D.) and again during the Sui Dynasty (seventh century A.D.). In fact, expeditions were probably sent to Taiwan earlier than this. During the Ch'in Dynasty (221 B.C. to 206 B.C.), the Emperor reportedly sent an expedition to I-chou--later identified as Taiwan.[14]

---

an impact on territorial claims within a number of nations and probably for that reason these claims cannot be disregarded altogether.

11. Historian Yu-ming Shaw makes this point. See Yu-ming Shaw, "Modern History of Taiwan: An Interpretative Account," in Hungdah Chiu (ed.), *China and the Taiwan Question* (New York: Praeger Publishers, 1979), p. 7.

12. See Simon Long, *Taiwan: China's Last Frontier* (New York: St. Martin's Press, 1991), p. 3.

13. See Ting-yee Kuo, "History of Taiwan," in Hungdah Chiu (ed.), *China and the Question of Taiwan: Documents and Analysis* (New York: Praeger Publishers, 1973), p. 4.

14. Hsu Fu is said to have been sent by the Emperor of the Ch'in Dynasty (221B.C. to 205 B.C.) to Taiwan. See Ting-yee Kuo, *General History of Taiwan* (Taipei: Cheng Chung Book Company, 1964), p. 2. Goodard also states that there may have

Other expeditions or visits, both before and after those cited by the authors could and should have been mentioned. In fact, a much better case for early contacts between China and Taiwan has been made by ROC historians.

Absent an argument that China made a claim to sovereignty over Taiwan or an explanation that the concept of sovereignty was not in use in China at this time, one might wonder why China did not exercise political control over Taiwan or why the leaders of these expeditions did not attempt to make Taiwan a part of China. The authors, by making the arguments they do, while not pointing out the absence of the concept of sovereignty in China at the time, create serious doubts about Taiwan's past links with China as they relate to a legal argument that Taiwan is part of China or should be thought of as Chinese territory.

The document proceeds to declare that since the early seventeenth century, "Chinese people began to step up the development of Taiwan." It does not mention, however, that the Chinese government never made any efforts to promote immigration to Taiwan or that the first settlers of Taiwan in modern history may have been Japanese.[15] Since these facts are known to most scholars of Taiwan, again the authors seem to be making a naive and perhaps counterproductive argument. Similarly, the authors do not say that Chinese who went to Taiwan did so in violation of the law in China. Again this is a historical fact. ROC historians have noted these issues, pointing out the fact that Peking espoused the policy it did toward Taiwan because of it being a government of non-Chinese (of Manchus from Manchuria) and its fear of anti-Manchu sentiment on the part of the Chinese there, and that Chinese culture and a loyalty and devotion to China remained with the Chinese on Taiwan even when the government paid little attention to them.[16]

Next the authors of the document observe that "their numbers (the Chinese population) topped one hundred thousand at the end of the

been Chinese migration to Taiwan during the period 770B.C. to 469 B.C. See Goodard, *Formosa: A Study in Chinese History,* p. 16.

15. See Shinkichi Ito, "An Outline of Formosan History," in Mark Mancall (ed.) *Formosa Today*, (New York: Praeger Publishers, 1963), p. 44.

16. Shaw, "Modern History of Taiwan: An Interpretative Account," Chiu (ed.), *China and the Taiwan Issue* p. 19.

century." And, "by 1893 their population exceeded 2.54 million." They, however, fail to note that Cheng Ch'eng-kung, better known in the West as Koxinga, who one ROC historian describes as the "great frontier developer," brought large number of Chinese immigrants to Taiwan--increasing the population to 100,000 by 1682.[17] Why do the authors fail to mention Cheng? Perhaps the reasons is this: Cheng, a Chinese nationalist or patriot, opposed the Manchu government in Peking, viewing it as a "foreign" dynasty. ROC historians, in addition to giving him credit for "making Taiwan Chinese," draw parallels between his rule and the ROC government which has opposed "foreign rule" in China (meaning that communism is alien to China, and, at least during the early years, the PRC was under the influence of the Soviet Union). This matter, which under ordinary conditions might be left for historians to debate, is highly sensitive in the PRC because of the widespread doubt about whether communism will survive in China and whether it was a mistake to adopt this foreign ideology in 1949.

In the "White Paper" is also found a list of different Chinese administrative bodies that ruled Taiwan "as early as the mid-twelfth century..." Here mention is made of Cheng Ch'eng-kung. But little more is said. Cheng fought numerous bloody battles against the Ch'ing or Manchu Dynasty government in an effort to restore the previous (Ming) dynasty which was Chinese. When he failed, he retreated to Taiwan and established a Chinese system of rule there with very little contact with China. His family would probably have continued to rule Taiwan for some time had not the Chinese army (note: under foreign control) invaded the island. In fact, it might be argued that he would have preserved Chinese culture there and might have attracted the loyalty of many Chinese on the mainland. Again the parallel between Cheng and the ROC quickly comes to mind.

Taiwan was subsequently ruled poorly by Beijing for some years. The authors do not want to mention this because it draws attention to the PRC today refusing to agree to a peaceful solution to the "Taiwan Question" and threatening to invade Taiwan. If that were to happen Taiwan would obviously be misruled under the PRC. In fact, prior to an invasion, if there were any warning, a million or two million people would probably flee Taiwan, causing a refugee problem in several other

---

17. See Wen-hsiung Hsu, "Chinese Colonization of Taiwan," PhD dissertation, University of Chicago, 1975, cited in Ibid, p. 11.

countries. Taiwan would then, no doubt, be put under military occupation. The democratization accomplished in Taiwan would be destroyed and Taiwan would be ruled in an authoritarian way again.

In 1885, the document points out, Taiwan was made a "full province covering three prefectures." The authors thus draw attention to the fact that China governed Taiwan for two centuries without making it a province. In fact, this is often cited by supporters of separation as evidence that China did not care about Taiwan. Taiwanese who advocate an independent Taiwan, in fact, use this as proof, along with details about the low character and quality of Chinese civil servants sent to Taiwan, corruption and statements in Chinese records about Taiwan being a place of rebellion and lacking civilization, as confirmation of the view that China did not think of Taiwan as part of China.[18] Statements made by the Chinese government to foreign governments at this time disclaiming responsibility for events that happened in Taiwan are seen as further testament that China did not claim sovereignty (a concept that had become almost universal by this time) over Taiwan.[19]

The fact that China was under foreign control at this time and, toward the end of the dynasty particularly, did not have the support of the people and was weak and in decline in large part explains this. The authors do not want to talk about this for reasons already mentioned. But there is no doubt another reason: because it was the "father" of the ROC, Sun Yat-sen, that liberated China from foreign rule. Sun also provided the thought and the inspiration behind Taiwan's economic and political development, which knowledgeable observers see as a momentous success in contrast to communism which failed the Chinese people in the PRC.

In describing Chinese rule, special mention is made of Liu Mingchuan (or Liu Ming-ch'uan as his name is romanized in Taiwan), the first governor of Taiwan and an enlightened official who brought railroads, mines, telegraph, merchant ships and schools to Taiwan. Says the document, "considerable social, economic and cultural

---

18. See Wen-hsiung Hsu, "Frontier Social Organization and Social Disorder in Ch'ing Taiwan," in Knapp (ed.), *China's Island Frontier*, p. 97.

19. See Lung-chu Chen and M.W. Reisman, "Who Owns Taiwan? A Search for International Title, " in Yung-huan Jo (ed.), *Taiwan's Future* (Tempe, Arizona: Center for Asian Studies, Arizona State University, 1974) for details.

advancement in Taiwan [were] achieved as a result." Actually, Taiwan experienced meaningful progress before this as a result of new economic policies that encouraged cash crops and foreign trade.[20] Similar policies were adopted by the government of the ROC after it was given jurisdiction over Taiwan after World War II. But, they were also policies the government of the PRC repudiated when it took political control of the mainland of China. Even more to the point, Taiwan became China's most advanced and most prosperous area at this time, just as it became China's most prosperous region under the ROC in the 1960s and after.

The recounting of Taiwan's history then jumps to 1945 when "the Chinese government reinstated its administrative authority in Taiwan Province." This, it says, was a product of "the Chinese people's victory in the war against Japanese aggression ..." An informed reader, when seeing this statement, may well be reminded that Mao Zedong (or Mao Tse-tung) had, several years earlier, put Taiwan in a category of nations or territory "outside of China." In fact, he placed Taiwan in the same category as Korea. Mao's words are worth re-quoting. He said:

It is the immediate task of China to regain all our lost territories, not merely to defend our sovereignty below the Great Wall. This means that Manchuria must be regained. We do not, however, include Korea, formerly a Chinese colony, but when we have reestablished the independence of the lost territories of China and if the Koreans wish to break away from the chains of Japanese imperialism, we will extend them our enthusiastic help. *The same thing applies for Formosa* [italics added].[21]

As indicated by this statement Mao did not think that Taiwan was part of China or Chinese territory. That being the case, we must conclude Mao contributed in an important way to the present problem. In contrast, the government of China--the Republic of China, or the same

---

20. For details, see Ramon H. Myers, "Taiwan under Ch'ing Imperial Rule: The Traditional Economy," *Journal of the Institute of Chinese Studies of the Chinese University of Hong Kong*, 5, No. 2. (1972), pp. 375-77.

21. See Edgar Snow, *Red Star Over China*, (New York: Random House, 1938), pp. 88-89.

government that rules Taiwan today--at this time *did* consider Taiwan territory belonging to China.

One may also wonder why the Chinese Communist Party (CCP) played no role in bringing Taiwan under Chinese sovereignty at this time. The Chinese government indeed "reinstated its ... authority" as the document reads in 1945; but the authors neglect to say it was the government of the Republic of China that did this. While the People's Republic of China did not yet exist, the Chinese Communist Party did, and it played a significant role in Chinese politics.[22] There were also contacts between the Chinese Communist Party and leaders in Taiwan. Yet the CCP had nothing to do with the "reinstatement" of Taiwan. Perhaps even more relevant, CCP leaders have frequently, and with considerable fanfare, taken credit for their successful guerrilla warfare efforts against the Japanese. Why did they not do anything in Taiwan? The Chinese Communist Party even failed to laud the return of Taiwan to Chinese sovereignty at the time.

The authors of the document go on to describe the struggle against foreign invasion by "Chinese on both sides of the Taiwan Straits [sic]." The intent is to put Taiwan and China "in the same boat" in terms of their relationship and experience with foreign powers. In reality, the experiences of the two were quite different. Taiwan was colonized; China was not. The fact that Taiwan was colonized, inasmuch as, according to international law, colonization was a legal process and sovereignty was put into the hands of the colonizing power, weakens significantly the historical argument that Taiwan was Chinese territory.

The writers then mention the conditions under which Japan colonized Taiwan. They cite "a thousand or more candidates (for the Imperial Examination) that protested the transfer of Taiwan to Japan via the Treaty of Shimonoseki and the fact that in Taiwan "people wailed and bemoaned the betrayal ..." If one reads between the lines of this argument, it appears that very few people in China knew or cared about Taiwan and the people in Taiwan had cause to feel betrayed by the Chinese government. The Chinese masses, of course, were unaware of these events due to the absence of mass communications and were, in

---

22. The reason, of course, may be that Taiwan was cut off from China before 1945. Still it is noteworthy that Mao had almost no influence in Taiwan at this time and seemed to have no interest either.

any event, not involved much in politics. The authors, however, appear to suggest they were. In doing so they are obviously assessing their history from a communist perspective and thus exhibit considerable naivete about the knowledge and influence of the Chinese masses historically. On the other hand, they may have adopted this line of argument deliberately to divert attention away from the real grounds for a Chinese claim to Taiwan--one that favors the ROC. More on this point below.

Then the document argues that "Taiwan compatriots never ceased their dauntless struggle throughout the Japanese occupation." In reality the Chinese population of Taiwan did not strongly oppose Japanese rule. Why? Early on, there was no central authority in Taiwan to organize a resistance movement once officials sent by the Chinese government left. In addition, the population of Taiwan had been living under conditions of warlordism, banditry, high crime rates and chaos, plus there was ethnic division among the Chinese population. Finally, the Chinese population was not armed and few had military training. Later, opinion was divided about Japanese rule; many judged Japanese rule to be efficient and honest, though it was exploitative and harsh. Hence, rather than having to cope with a problem of those "never ceasing their dauntless struggle," Japan found it rather easy to govern Taiwan and experienced little opposition or protest, especially when compared to its rule of Korea.[23] The United States in large part decided against an invasion of Taiwan in 1945, calculating that the local population would fight with Japan rather than rise against their Japanese rulers.[24]

The authors' assessment should have mentioned that the population of Taiwan was not absorbed or assimilated by Japan even though this was Tokyo's stated policy for some time. This means the people of Taiwan could not be made Japanese. This was quite unlike the

---

23. See George H. Kerr, *Formosa: Licensed Revolution and the Home Rule Movement, 1895-1945* (Honolulu: University of Hawaii Press, 1975), p. 13. Kerr is known to be sympathetic with the Taiwanese population as opposed to the government and his works have often been cited by supporters of independence; nevertheless, neither his scholarship nor the arguments being cited here have been questioned seriously.

24. See George H. Kerr, *Formosa Betrayed* (Boston: Houghton-Mifflin Co., 1965), Chapter 2.

situation in the Ryukyu Islands.[25]   In short, Chinese culture survived in Taiwan notwithstanding Japanese efforts to erase it.

The authors then argue that "the international community has acknowledged the fact that Taiwan belongs to China." In making this argument they cite the Cairo Declaration of 1943 and the Potsdam Proclamation of 1945. In the Cairo Declaration, three powers--the United States, Great Britain and China (the Republic of China)-- declared that "it is their purpose that territory taken by Japan shall be returned." While these documents had legal standing they did not have the broad support of the international community as the authors suggest. At the time the Cairo Declaration was concluded most nations of the world were preoccupied with other issues and paid little attention to this matter. Moreover, the end of the war was not near. The Potsdam Proclamation contained an affirmation of what was stated in the Cairo Declaration. But again, few nations stated any opinion in support of (though they certainly didn't oppose) its provisions about Taiwan.

Viewing these two wartime declarations as the legal basis for the return of Taiwan to China presents other problems. First, while such declarations are considered legitimate by most international legal scholars, they provide comparatively weak evidence under international law for a claim of sovereignty. In addition, it is questionable whether these "wartime pronouncements" could override provisions in the Treaty of Shimonoseki, which provided for the transfer of sovereignty over Taiwan to Japan.[26] Second, at the time, most observers regarded the problem as one that would be resolved formally via a pending peace treaty with Japan. In fact, this would probably have happened had the PRC not objected to being left out of the peace conference. In any event, the issue was left technically unresolved. The United States subsequently took the position that the matter had not legally been decided, but that the government of the

---

25. See Kerr, *Formosa: Licensed Revolution and the Home Rule Movement*, p. 161-68. The author also notes that Japan's *kominka* or assimilation policy worked better among the Aborigines.

26. See Hungdah Chiu, "China, the United States and the Question of Taiwan," in Hungdah Chiu (ed.), *China and the Question of Taiwan: Documents and Analysis*, (New York: Praeger Publishers, 1973), p. 134 for further analysis on this point.

Republic of China "effectively controls" Taiwan and the Pescadores.[27] Most other nations of the world, and legal scholars alike, did not contradict the U.S. position.

More important than these wartime declarations is the fact that Japan abdicated jurisdiction and sovereignty over Taiwan in 1945 and at the same time transferred Taiwan to the Republic of China. Tokyo, in fact, negotiated with the Nationalist side, or the Republic of China, while it was involved in a civil war, giving the impression that it regarded it as the legally constituted government notwithstanding the challenge to its authority by the Chinese Communists. And, while there was no legal document to support this transfer and to whom the transfer was made was unclear, it may be easily assumed that it was to the Republic of China since its administrative personnel and troops managed the transfer.[28] Later the Japanese government seemed to confirm the correctness or the legality of its action when it signed a peace treaty with the Republic of China, even though the People's Republic of China existed at the time and governed the mainland, or most of China.

The People's Republic of China, of course, makes claim to be the successor government of the Republic of China. In fact, much of what is said in this document is predicated on that position. This being the case, some comments are in order concerning the strength of that position. A main principle of international law is this: a successor state argument is fatally weakened if the other government still exists. Thus, inasmuch as the Republic of China still exists, and still is a sovereign nation-state, the successor government argument cannot be regarded as valid or meaningful. Indeed, how can there be a successor government to a government that is alive and well?[29]

---

27. This was stated in a letter by Secretary of State John Foster Dulles to George K.C. Yeh, Minister of Foreign Affairs of the Republic of China dated December 10, 1954. See Hungdah Chiu (ed.), *China and the Question of Taiwan* (New York: Praeger Publishers, 1973), p. 252-3.

28. Japanese scholars have taken this position. See Chiu (ed), *China and the Question of Taiwan*, *p*. 136.

29. It is also worth noting that the U.S., as well as most other nations, take the view that it is required that they treat a regime in effective control of a territory as a government and that this applies to the ROC. See Hungdah Chiu, "The

That the ROC has governed Taiwan since 1945 and has been a stable government with strong public support in recent years would also support--many would say in a crucial way--the argument of it having title to Taiwan.[30] This argument is bolstered by the ROC being regarded by most experts as one of, if not *the* country in the world, in terms of economic success and one of the few that, while promoting economic growth, almost totally eliminated poverty and reduced the disparity of income and wealth of its citizens. In addition, in recent years, Taiwan has democratized very quickly, perhaps faster than any other nation in the world. Hence, it is difficult to say that the ROC should not, for reasons of how it has ruled Taiwan and the support it has from the population, be viewed as legitimate.

A case can, of course, be made that Taiwan should be independent. And such a case is made by certain groups including the major opposition party, the Democratic Progressive Party. In fact, the DPP has made this argument on many occasions. It made it during election campaigns in 1986 and 1989. Leading up to the 1991 election DPP leaders made it a plank in the party's platform. As well, opposition party members have made the case for an independent Taiwan to the public frequently by other means. In part, their claim is based on historical arguments that are much different and are at odds with those used by the authors of the "White Paper." The independence advocates often cite weak historical ties, the lack of a formal transfer from Japan to the ROC and the unpopularity of a ROC government as reflected by a "revolution" against that government in February 1947.[31] If one discounts the fact that the ROC has ruled Taiwan since World War II and has engineered miracle economic growth and impressive social and political development (meaning democratization as was noted in the above paragraph), the independence argument might be quite convincing.[32]

International Law of Recognition and the Status of the Republic of China," in Steven W. Mosher (ed.), *The United States and the Republic of China: Democratic Friends, Economic Partners* (New Brunswick: Transaction Press, 1992), p. 15.

30. See Chiu (ed), *China and the Question of Taiwan*, pp. 171-76.

31. See Chen and Reisman, "Who Owns Taiwan? for further details.

32. Advocates of Taiwan independence also make the case that a plebiscite should be held in Taiwan to decide the island's future. There is precedent for this, of course. The government's position, supported by the ruling KMT, is that in a

In making the case they do, the authors of this document appear to be, wittingly or otherwise, supporting the cause of Taiwan independence by giving great stress to the historical argument, when the historical evidence or historical arguments fail to convince many of an incontrovertible Chinese territorial claim, and, in any event, have little weight in international law today. They also draw attention to the historical arguments made by independence advocates when the real case for Chinese sovereignty over Taiwan (and thus for a one-China policy) stems instead from the fact that Japan gave up sovereignty and made a transfer of its legal authority over Taiwan to the Republic of China and the ROC has governed Taiwan and adjacent territories continuously and successfully since 1945--almost half a century.

The writers appear to carry on the discourse they do in order to weaken the argument that Taiwan belongs to the Republic of China. They ostensibly do this because they realize that their claim to be the successor government, and, therefore, the legal owner of Taiwan is undefensible if not completely lacking in merit. Yet, by so doing, they help support the argument of those who say that Taiwan is not part of China. In essence, they are contributing to the separatist position.

III

In chapter two of the "White Paper" the authors argue that Taiwan was "returned to China *de jure* and *de facto* at the end of the Second World War." There is no question that it was returned *de facto*; no one has ever questioned that. What the writers failed to mention, however, is that transfer was made to the Nationalist Chinese government or the Republic of China. Whether it was made *de jure* at the time is the subject of some question as well as considerable debate as was noted above.

As was also already mentioned, there was no document that formalized the transfer; rather Japan evacuated the island having lost the war and having accepted the relevant provisions in the Cairo

democratic system this is unnecessary and Taiwan is now a democracy, and most Western observers agree with this argument as reflected by the fact the Western media doesn't mention or advocate anymore, at least very often, that a plebiscite be held in Taiwan. The government also cites public opinion surveys on the issue, which may be seen as an informal plebescite.

Declaration and the Potsdam Proclamation. Hence, many argue that there was no legal transfer at the time. The reason this happened may simply be because the U.S. planned to occupy the island after an invasion and until a peace treaty could be signed, but, for reasons of military strategy, skipped Taiwan and attacked Okinawa instead.[33] If one chooses to argue that the peace treaty subsequently signed between Tokyo and Taipei in 1952 does not constitute a legal transfer (since it does not mention any new ownership of Taiwan specifically, though one might infer that), then Taiwan ostensibly became property of the Republic of China through the *de facto* transfer of authority plus occupation over time--from 1945 to the present.[34] In either case it would appear the Republic of China gained legal claim to jurisdiction and sovereignty over Taiwan.

The ROC, in addition, may claim sovereignty over Taiwan on the basis of prescription (a claim to territory based on the uncontested exercise of control over an extended period of time), since the PRC has never taken any specific or significant actions to recover Taiwan, but rather has limited such efforts to the Offshore Islands only.[35] Prescription is also a sound legal basis for a territorial claim according to the current practice in international law.[36]

---

33. See Franz H. Michael and George E. Taylor, *The Far East and the Modern World* (New York: Holt, Rinehart and Winston, 1964), p. 448.

34. The treaty states that "Japan has renounced all right, title and claim to Taiwan and Penghu." It goes on to say that "all treaties, conventions and agreements concluded before December 9, 1941, between China and Japan have become null and void ..." Thus the Treaty of Shimonoseki, by which Taiwan was ceded to Japan, was canceled. Hence, one could argue that Japan did make a legal transfer of Taiwan to the Republic of China. See Chiu, *China, the United States and the Question of Taiwan,* op cit., p. 127 for further details.

35. In the 1950s, two crises resulted from PRC efforts to seize the Offshore Islands. However, PRC forces in neither case attacked Taiwan or the Pescadores or made a parallel effort to take Taiwan by force. Thus, one might argue that the ROC's sovereignty over the Offshore Islands has been contested, but not the rest of its territory.

36. It might also be noted that only the government of the Republic of China has truly governed the entire island of Taiwan. As late as 1942, it was reported that 44 percent of the island's land surface was called "Aborigine territory" and the

What is written in this document is clearly a biased case rather than an effort to argue from the point of international law--though at times the authors couch their arguments in legal terms. That they ignore many important legal points, however, is quite noticeable to any knowledgeable reader, not to mention a prime weakness in their line of argument.

The authors, to further contend (departing from the legal line of argument) that the Republic of China is an illegitimate government, comment on the history of the civil war between the Nationalists and the Communists before 1949. They cite a "reign of terror" as one of the reasons the Nationalists lost the war. This argument is of questionable merit, however, because of lack of proof regarding who was the most ruthless and cruel participant in the Chinese Civil War. Most historians say the Communists were. Moreover, new historical evidence suggests that the Communists won the struggle in large part because they engaged in a reign of terror that far exceeded any atrocities the Nationalists might have committed and did things that have been described as "beyond the imagination" of most people.[37]

Japanese colonial government maintained only weak control over it and left some parts of it unattended. See George H, Kerr, *Formosa: Licensed Revolution and the Home Rule Movement, 1895-1945*, pp. 105-6.

37. Most scholars writing on this period have described the actions of the Chinese Communist Party during this period as reflecting brutality and determination to win, regardless of the consequences in terms of loss of life. A recent publication further underscores the CCP's brutality. In Lt. Col. Zhang Zheng-long's recently published book entitled *Xuebai Xuehong* (White Snow, Red Blood) describing the civil war in Manchuria in 1947, the author, quoting secret war reports and eyewitnesses, says that the Communists employed a strategy of starving the population of a city of one-half million in order to burden the Nationalists. He says they unnecessarily killed as many as 150,000 people in that way. The book was immediately banned and President Yang Shangkun singled it out for criticism and Zhang was arrested. For further details, see John F. Copper and Ta-ling Lee, *Tiananmen Aftermath: Human Rights in the People's Republic of China, 1990* (Baltimore: University of Maryland School of Law, 1992), p. 67. It is also worthy of note that in North Korean President Kim Il Sung's 1992 autobiography, Kim says that during the Japanese occupation, Chinese Communists "murdered" more than 2,000 Korean party members and tortured others. See "Washington Whispers," *U.S. News and World Reports*, June

Hence one of the themes in the document is seriously undermined by both facts that have been known for a long time and some that have become rather widely known through the publication of recent works on the subject.

The authors also assert that the Nationalists were "spurned by the people"--saying that this was another reason for the Nationalist's defeat. The implication, of course, is that the Communist "revolution" was a popular one and through support of the masses the Communists acceded to power. Most evidence, however, seems to indicate that (and Western historians certainly make this argument) strategic and tactical mistakes on the part of the Nationalist armies and astute tactics and tough fighting on the part of the Communists gave them victory--a military victory. Hence, there was no popular revolution.[38]

After this victory, so says the document, the "new People's Republic became the sole legal government of China." Since the government of the Republic of China was not rendered extinct at this juncture, having moved to Taiwan, the authors seem to suggest that Taiwan was not part of China, at that time at least. This point may seem trivial except for the fact that Mao is reported to have said later that it was a mistake to adopt the name "People's Republic of China," inasmuch as they (meaning he and his victorious Red Army and the Chinese Communist Party) might have used the term Republic of China and claimed successfully to be the successor regime, the Nationalists having been defeated.[39] Alternatively, he might have proclaimed the

---

27, 1994, p. 24.

38. See A. Doak Barnett, *China on the Eve of Communist Takeover* (New York: Praeger Publishers, 1963), p. 63. Barnett says: "The actual pattern of Communist takeover in China hardly fit into traditional Marxist concepts .... It was not an urban insurrection, a coup d'etat, or even, for that matter a general peasant revolt. Instead, the pattern was one of systematic military conquest--or in the latter stages, of negotiated surrender imposed by the Communists, who by then had achieved clear military predominance."

39. In November 1989, the PRC released a document that revealed that there were many advocates of retaining the title Republic of China in the early days of the PRC. This same document records that Mao told Edgar Snow in October 1970 that he regretted the name change. See *United Daily News* (Taipei), November 9, 1989, p. 4. Underscoring the fact this idea was still alive, in late 1993, Wang Daohan, head of the PRC's Association for Relations Across the Taiwan Strait

civil war still unfinished. Instead he chose to change the name of the nation, and, in so doing, allowed the Republic of China to remain a legal entity (since it was not rendered extinct but rather continued to exist) and in a sense made Taiwan, temporarily at least, separate from China. Back to this point later.

The authors proceed to discuss U.S. responsibility for the "Taiwan question"--saying essentially that the United States caused or created this problem. They contend that the U.S. provided money, weapons and advisors to carry on the civil war and block the advance of the Chinese people's revolution. While there is truth in this statement, it is also a fact that the U.S. withheld support to the Nationalists in order to encourage negotiations and in some important senses remained neutral.[40] Clearly the U.S. did not have leverage over the Communists, so when it reduced or stopped support of the Nationalists, these actions encouraged Communist leaders to continue the fighting. Washington, in fact, was put in a difficult position in terms of taking actions that would end the fighting--which was American policy. The Marshall Mission sent to China at this time, of course, sought to end the conflict.[41] The U.S., however, made no serious effort to control or extinguish, lacking both the will and the wherewithal, what might be

said that Beijing was willing to negotiate with Taiwan on a host of issues-- including the national title. See *United Daily News*, November 12, 1993, p. 10.

This issue is discussed at length in the following sources: Peter Kien-hong Yu, "Establishing a Federated New China," *Chung-kuo Ta-lu (China Mainland)*, August 1994 and Peter Kien-hong Yu, "Toward a Republic of Taiwan or Republic of China: A Hypothetical Analysis," (Paper presented at the American Association of Chinese Studies annual meeting in October 1992). The author also argues that PRC leaders have recently debated the issue of changing the name of the country from the People's Republic of China to the Republic of China. See Peter Kien-hong Yu, "Moving toward a new Republic of China," *China News* (Taipei), June 30, 1993, p. 7.

40. See Tang Tsou, *America's Failure in China, 1941-50, Vol. 1* (Chicago: University of Chicago Press, 1963), chapter IV.

41. Marshall was instructed not to interfere in China's internal affairs. And President Truman said at the time that the United States support would not involve any effort to influence China's internal situation. For details, see David M. Finkelstein, *Washington's Taiwan Dilemma: From Abandonment to Salvation* (Fairfax, Virginia: George Mason University Press, 1993), p. 27.

called "revolutionary" forces. Anyway, the civil war was won on the battlefield according to most historians.

All of this may be begging the question. Since neither Mao nor any other leader of the Chinese Communist Party expressed any interest in Taiwan until 1949, this discussion, at least as it pertains to what happened in China in the years immediately after 1945, could well be deemed irrelevant.

After the Korean War started in 1950, as the authors state, the United States intervened to prevent an invasion of Taiwan, which would have ended the Chinese Civil War. True. However, the United States also prevented what would have been extensive damage to Taiwan and considerable loss of life.[42] Moreover, this action by the United States and the subsequent signing of a defense pact with the Republic of China brought stability to Taiwan, and, according to many scholars, was vital to the economic and political development that followed. It eventually brought to Taiwan democracy and respect for human rights (which, incidently, many say the PRC should emulate). In this light, it is difficult to accuse the U.S. of wrongdoing in the sense of causing harm to the Chinese people. It is also incorrect to say that the United States had "imperialist" designs on Taiwan; clearly the evidence doesn't support this and no serious historian has ever made this claim. Furthermore, Chinese leaders in Beijing have taken the position that the U.S. did not intend to maintain a presence in Taiwan or to occupy the island.[43]

The writers go on to say that no progress was made on "easing and removing tension in the Taiwan Straits [sic] area" during the 1950s and early and mid-60s. Clearly the U.S. sought to prevent conflict in the area and acted otherwise only when the Nationalist-held territories

---

42. An invasion of Taiwan by PRC forces has been estimated to result in high casualties--a million or more--by a number of authors.

The book *August 1995: China's Violent Invasion of Taiwan* by Chen Lang-ping published in 1994 in Taiwan describes this in quite scary language. The fact it became an instant best-seller indicates that the population of Taiwan is concerned, perhaps scared, of this possibility.

43. In the mid-1980s, Deng Xiaoping suggested the PRC would use military force against Taiwan under several circumstances, including *"if Taipei leaned toward Moscow instead of Washington."* (Italics added.) See Guo-cang Huan, "Taiwan: A View from Beijing," *Foreign Affairs*, Summer 1985, p. 1068.

of Quemoy and Matsu were attacked by military forces of the People's Republic of China. Washington, as the records show, attempted to restrain the ROC and its military forces as reflected in its signals to Taipei not to take provocative action against PRC forces and in efforts to persuade the ROC government to reduce its forces on the islands.[44] Subsequently, U.S. military assistance to the ROC was almost exclusively defensive weapons. This is well documented.

According to the "White Paper," a breakthrough occurred in the late 1960s and early 1970s "when the international situation had undergone changes and as New China had gained in strength ..." Apparently reference is made to Washington's new policy iterated in 1969 in the Nixon Doctrine, a policy designed to extricate the U.S. from Vietnam with the PRC's help. In this connection it should be noted that American and other scholars have pointed out that Beijing did not ultimately help the United States: North Vietnam did not abide by the peace treaty and invaded the south and destroyed the government of South Vietnam, ultimately causing immense suffering and human rights abuses. Thus, one may put it this way: the United States, in a *quid pro quo* for a promise the PRC made to help the U.S. get out of Vietnam (but a promise it did not later fulfill), came to Beijing's rescue at this very time--when the People's Republic of China was being threatened by the Soviet Union during and following a border "war" over Damansky Island in the Usurri River.[45] Most observers believe that the PRC was very seriously threatened and that it had to change its relationship with the United States (the only other superpower) to deal with threats from Moscow to "take out" Beijing's nuclear weapons and missile sites and/or invade China and change the government in Beijing.[46]

---

44. In fact, the U.S. as early as 1954 pressured Taipei to reduce its offensive military capabilities and agree not to take offensive action against the PRC without U.S. concurrence. See A. Doak Barnett, *Communist China and Asia: A Challenge to American Policy* (New York: Vintage Books, 1960), p. 411.

45. For details, see John F. Copper, *China Diplomacy: The Washington-Taipei-Beijing Triangle* (Boulder: Westview Press, 1992), pp. 31-34.

46. Clearly China was not in a position militarily to cope with the Soviet threat. It is noteworthy that Lin Biao, who may have instigated the conflict for political reasons relating to his role as Mao's successor, saw his power diminish after

Hence, it is hardly accurate to say that U.S. policy was to a large extent motivated by the fact that "New China had gained in strength." Patently the PRC was in a difficult position at this time and wanted to negotiate with the United States, and did. Recall that Mao had promised many times never to negotiate with the United States until the "Taiwan question" had been resolved. Mao, in short, ate this promise because of the Soviet military threat.

U.S. President Richard Nixon's visit in February 1972 followed this, though the authors chose to link it to the "lawful rights" of the People's Republic of China being "restored" in the United Nations rather than simply to power politics. However, doubt is cast on their argument by Henry Kissinger's visit to Beijing in July 1971 and the announcement of the Nixon trip, both of which happened before discussions and debate on China's representation in the United Nations and prior to the date Beijing entered the U.N. and "representatives of the Taiwan authorities" were "expelled."[47]

In any event, during President Nixon's visit, he and his Chinese hosts, on behalf of the United States and the People's Republic of China respectively, signed a joint communique in Shanghai that became known as the Shanghai Communique. As the authors note, the United States, in that communique, "acknowledged" that "all Chinese on either side of the Taiwan Strait maintain that there is but one China and that Taiwan is a part of China." Thus, they conclude that the U.S. unequivocally supported the PRC's position on Taiwan. Western analysts, however, have noted the use of the word "acknowledge" is a weak term diplomatically and point out that the term "agree" might have been employed. Use of the expression "acknowledge," in fact, seems to reflect both an intentional ambiguity and an unwillingness to make a clear promise or a more solid commitment. The subsequent use of the word "either," to ostensibly mean both, which is not proper English, further indicates the U.S. was

---

that, probably as a result of the conflict. For further details, see Harold C. Hinton, *The Sino-Soviet Confrontation: Implications for the Future* (New York: Crane Russak & Company, Inc., 1976), chapter 3.

47. Actually, the ROC was not expelled from the United Nations. Rather it withdrew when it was realized that Beijing would be given the China seat after a vote to decide whether it was an "important question" or not.

not serious about this provision.[48] Others argue that the statement also contains a blatant lie: that "all Chinese ... maintain there is but one China." Clearly if these words are taken to mean that Taiwan should be ruled by Beijing, then it is not only false to say that all Chinese agree: the overwhelming majority of Chinese in Taiwan did not agree. It might also be noted that if one reads the entire document, the two countries state positions which mostly disagree with the other and that in seeking common ground and finding a resolution to the "Taiwan issue" impossible, they talked about Taiwan only in ambiguous language and no specific promises of action were made.[49]

The authors then describe the process by which the United States and the People's Republic of China agree to establish formal diplomatic relations in late 1978 (effective January 1, 1979). They point out that the United States accepted three conditions set forth by the Chinese government: sever "diplomatic relations" (with the Republic of China), abrogate the "mutual defense treaty," and withdraw military forces from Taiwan. They do not mention that the United States also set forth conditions: a peaceful solution only to the Taiwan question and the continuation of arms sales to Taiwan.[50] The Carter Administration did not demand that these conditions be put in writing so as not to embarrass Deng Xiaoping and to avoid the appearance of a U.S. two-China policy. But the U.S. did set conditions, and for good reason.[51]

---

48. See Copper, *China Diplomacy*, pp. 34-39.

49. Ibid.

50. See Department of State's News Release entitled "Diplomatic Relations with the People's Republic of China and Future Relations with Taiwan," (Washington D.C.: Bureau of Public Affairs, 1978).

51. Carter's national security advisor argued that the continuation of arms sales was necessary to prevent Taiwan from exercising the Soviet or nuclear "options." See Zbigniew Brezinski, *Power and Principle*, (New York: Farrar, Straus and Giroux, 1983), p 218. Other officials contended that it would prevent a PRC attack on the island and maintain U.S. foreign policy credibility. See Jaw-ling Joanne Chang, *United States-China Normalization: An Evaluation of Foreign Policy Decision Making*, (Denver: University of Denver Monograph Series in World Affairs, No. 4, 1986), p. 86.

The authors, while avoiding any mention of U.S. conditions, do mention that the United States "will maintain cultural, commercial and other unofficial relations with the people of Taiwan." But, they do not interpret this statement. Some observers have seen this clause as reflecting a change from a two-Chinas to a one-China, one-Taiwan policy on the part of the U.S. Others say it simply meant the U.S. was downgrading its relations with Taipei. The opinion has also been expressed that it meant that President Carter sought to avoid ignoring Taiwan completely. Still others have argued that it was an invitation to Congress to help resolve the matter. Clearly, this statement, once noted, should have been given some interpretation. One might think the authors did not do this to avoid drawing attention to the fact that the U.S. Congress reversed this policy in writing the Taiwan Relations Act.[52]

The authors also cite the fact that the U.S. "acknowledges" that there is only one China and that Taiwan is part of China. Again, while true, it is noteworthy that the U.S. side used a vague and non-committal term when a much stronger word such as "agrees" might have been employed. One wonders why it was not.

The Carter Administration, it must be noted, conducted the negotiations in secret, not only from the public but Congress as well, in order to avoid disruptive debate that certainly would have ensued. Also the agreement was kept extremely brief to avoid controversy.[53] Thus, the White House failed to address many serious questions concerning Washington-Taipei relations and it was obvious that the Congress would step in and fill the void; in fact, President Carter expected this.[54] Chinese leaders in Beijing must have understood this. But they went ahead with normalization anyway. The explanation may be that the PRC was about to go to war with Vietnam and wanted to resolve the issue of diplomatic relations with the U.S. before that. This, however, seems more a rationalization than a valid explanation.

---

52. See Copper, *China Diplomacy*, pp. 39-41.

53. The Normalization Agreement is less than three hundred words in length. It contains very few details on any aspect of U.S.-China relations, especially Taiwan, and does not appear to recognize problems in U.S.-ROC relations that needed to be considered.

54. The Carter Administration, in fact, prepared draft legislation which it sent to Congress in January.

Chinese negotiators dealing with U.S. matters were not really distracted by the PRC's war with Vietnam as reflected by the fact they tendered a protest about the Taiwan Relations Act and issued numerous other statements about U.S.-China relations at this time. It also seems relevant that at this juncture Beijing reported quite a number of positive things about Sino-U.S. relations.[55] In any event, the war did not last long.

The authors of the document then talk of the "so-called Taiwan Relations Act" passed by the Congress and signed by the President "scarcely three months after ..." They state that the TRA "contravened the communique on the establishment of diplomatic relations between China and the U.S. and the principles of international law, and seriously prejudiced the rights and interests of the Chinese people." The TRA indeed "contravened" the Normalization Agreement in the sense that it returned, in the view of the U.S., to the ROC (though the term Taiwan was used throughout) its sovereignty--since it treated it as a legally constituted nation-state in a number of important ways. For example, Taiwan was allowed to use U.S. courts as other nations do, while the issues of property, debts and contracts were treated in the same way as dealing with any other legally constituted sovereign nation-state. U.S. Immigration and Naturalization Law still applied as it did to other nations. Taiwan's diplomats were given diplomatic immunity. And the United States, via the Taiwan Relations Act, promised security protection to Taipei and expressed a concern for democracy and human rights in Taiwan. It seems undeniable that the U.S. Congress, in the course of writing the TRA, assumed Taipei possessed sovereignty even though the law studiously avoided using the term Republic of China to not contradict President Carter's China policy in too blatant a fashion.[56]

This, however, is again something that leaders of the People's Republic of China should have, and no doubt did, anticipate. It was done in an open, careful, democratic and legal manner over a period of three months. Moreover, Chinese officials from the PRC Embassy in

---

55. For further details, see Gene T. Hsiao, "A Renewed Crisis over Taiwan and Its Impact on Sino-American Relations," in Gene T. Hsiao and Michael Witunski (eds.), *Sino-American Normalization and its Policy Implications* (New York: Praeger Publishers, 1983), pp. 84-85.

56. See Copper, *China Diplomacy*, p. 23 for further details.

Washington, D.C. attended the hearings daily. When President Carter signed the bill, making it law, officials in Beijing delivered a note to Ambassador Woodcock saying it was "unacceptable." However, no threats or ultimatums were made and the official protest was not threatening.[57] If it were really seen as a serious violation of the rights and interests of the Chinese people, the PRC government certainly should have objected vigorously and perhaps might even have considered the Normalization Agreement null and void. Finally it would appear odd that U.S.-China relations improved very markedly, which they did, if Beijing had serious reservations about U.S. Taiwan policy.

According to President Jimmy Carter, he communicated with Chinese leaders on these and other issues that were raised by the TRA. Chinese officials, according to President Carter, did not object to the defense pact with the ROC remaining in force for a year as well as other U.S. treaties and agreements signed with the ROC (and not just effective for one more year, but rather indefinitely).[58] He also notes that PRC leaders were told that the United States would make a unilateral statement that the United States expected differences between China and Taiwan would be resolved peacefully yet Beijing went ahead with normalization anyway.[59]

It is instructive to quote relevant provisions of the Taiwan Relations Act that the PRC thinks "contravene" the Normalization Agreement, especially those pertaining to Taiwan's legal status. Taking cognizance of these provisions that were written into U.S. law by the Congress, one might think that Beijing should have regarded the Normalization Agreement as having been nullified in large part, or, at least contradicted by the TRA, and should have called for renegotiations or should have at least pressured the United States to change it. The relevant provisions of the Taiwan Relations Act are worth quoting:

---

57. See Copper, *China Diplomacy*, p. 68 for further details.

58. This, in fact, struck some observers as very odd--especially the fact that from the PRC perspective it was allowing the U.S. to maintain a defense pact with what it considered to be province of the PRC for a year.

59. See President Carter's news conference of January 17, 1979, in *Public Papers of the Presidents, 1979, Vol 1*, pp. 50 and 53.

Sec. 4 (b)

(1) Whenever the laws of the United States refer or relate to foreign countries, nations, states, governments, or similar entities, such terms shall include and such laws shall apply with respect to Taiwan ....

(3) (a) The absence of diplomatic relations and recognition with respect to Taiwan shall not abrogate, infringe, modify, or deny or otherwise affect in any way rights or obligations (including but not limited to those involving contracts, debts, or property interests of any kind) under the laws of the United States heretofore or hereafter acquired by or with respect to Taiwan ....

(7) The capacity of Taiwan to sue and be sued in courts in the United States, in accordance with the laws of the United States ... shall not be abrogated, infringed, modified, denied, or otherwise affected in any way by the absence of diplomatic relations or recognition.

(8) No requirement ... under the laws of the United States with respect to maintenance of diplomatic relations or recognition shall be applicable with respect to Taiwan.

Sec. 4 (c) For the purposes, including in any court in the United States, the Congress approves the continuation in force of all treaties and other international agreements ... entered into by the United States and the governing authorities on Taiwan ... prior to 1 January 1979 ....

Sec. 4 (d) Nothing in this Act may be construed as a basis for supporting exclusion or expulsion of Taiwan from continued membership in any... international organization.

Next the authors look at the August Communique, or "Shanghai II," negotiated by the United States and the People's Republic of China in 1982 to resolve the issue of arms sales to Taiwan. They observe that the United States declared that it "does not seek to carry out a long-term policy of arms sales ..., that its arms sales ... will not exceed ... the level of those supplied in recent years ...." They, however, neglect to mention several points: One, the Normalization Agreement was made with the condition that arms sales to Taiwan would continue. Two, the matter of arms sales to Taiwan was put in the Taiwan Relations Act and made "the law of the land" in the United States and could not legally be superseded by a communique. Three, the communique in question was predicated upon a "peaceful solution only" pledge by the People's Republic of China. Looking at the August Communique in this context, one might wonder if it really meant what it said or was negotiated for some other purpose--namely to succor Deng Xiaoping, who at the time was experiencing serious domestic political problems. Deng was under pressure from hard-liners who (given the fact Deng was a nationalist, as opposed to being a communist ideologue, and was, therefore, vulnerable to criticism on territorial issues) were attacking Deng for abandoning Taiwan for better relations with the United States.[60]

The Subcommittee on Separation of Powers of the Committee (Senate) of the Judiciary subsequently examined the question of conflict between the communique and the Taiwan Relations Act. Its report noted that the administration insisted that "the joint communique was not an executive agreement or an international agreement giving rise to legal rights and legal obligations." Assistant Secretary of State Holdridge described it as a *"modus vivendi."* Legal Advisor Robinson called it a "statement of expectations." Winston Lord, who later became Assistant Secretary of State for Asia and the Pacific, portrayed it as "a framework for managing our differences with the Chinese over a matter of great sensitivity to us both."[61]

---

60. Many scholars of PRC politics not only note that Deng is a pragmatist, but also that he has sought to push his reforms by promoting China's past greatness, which he wants to restore--thus he is called a nationalist. This point, and its relationship to the issue of territory, will be discussed again below.

61. *Report on the Taiwan Relations Act and the Joint Communique* (Washington, DC: U.S. Government Printing Office, June 1983). It is also worth noting that on April 30, 1994, U.S. President Clinton signed a bill (A Department of State Authorization bill) with an amendment attached that reaffirmed the precedence of the TRA to this and other communiques signed with the PRC.

Many Western analysts have seen the August Communique as an effort by the United States to bolster the reformist government of Deng Xiaoping rather than a statement of policy or a legal commitment. It clearly evoked disagreement, rather than consensus, about the legality of arms sales to Taiwan at the time, since it appeared to violate the Taiwan Relations Act, which was superior to it in legal terms (since the TRA was a law established by Congress, whereas the communique was not approved by another branch of government). Moreover, the communique was not signed. Comments about it afterwards, including President Reagan's statement that it was predicated upon a peaceful settlement (of the Taiwan question) pledge by the Chinese government (which Deng said he didn't make) are cause for questioning both the nature and the purpose of the agreement. U.S. Department of State personnel later testifying before Congressional committees created further doubt about the communique's status. In September, for example, Davis Robinson, a Department of State legal advisor, told a subcommittee of the Senate Judiciary Committee that the communique is not an international agreement and thus imposes no obligation to either party under international law.[62]

The writers go on to note that the sale of 150 F-16 fighter aircraft by the U.S. to Taiwan in 1992 violated the agreement. Clearly, that appears to be the case. Yet the government of the United States said at the time that it did not. And Beijing did not refute Washington's position. In fact, the PRC said very little about the sale of aircraft to Taiwan when it was announced. There was no loud protest; nor was there any significant punitive action taken against the United States. Beijing temporarily boycotted "Big Five" talks on nuclear proliferation in the Middle East and rejected a proposal for a Chinese-American human rights commission. But this was not earthshaking. And offsetting, even undermining, these actions (assuming they were designed to express displeasure with the U.S.) the PRC at this time made a large purchase of American wheat and bought six Boeing aircraft. Apparently Chinese leaders in Beijing excused the U.S. action as necessary for President Bush to be reelected.[63] Bush's reelection was

---

62. See Martin L. Lasater, *U.S. Interests in the New Taiwan* (Boulder: Westview Press, 1993), p. 21.

63. See Dennis VanVranken Hickey, *United States-Taiwan Security Ties: From Cold War to Beyond Containment* (Westport, CT: Praeger Publishers, 1994), p. 89.

considered important to the People's Republic of China. PRC actions at this time, in fact, reflected favoritism toward Bush over candidate Bill Clinton, which incidently could have been construed as interference in the domestic affairs of the United States (which most nations carefully avoid doing and the PRC has so often condemned when it thinks another country is meddling in its internal affairs).

Most U.S. leaders, like many Western scholars, took the position that the sale was necessary to maintain the balance of power in the Taiwan Strait in view of the People's Republic of China engaging in a rapid military build-up. It expanded its defense budget and bought aircraft and other weapons in very significant quantity and quality from the former Soviet Union.[64] Even candidate Bill Clinton iterated this position at the time.[65] Some observers also said that Beijing's military buildup violated provisions of the Shanghai Communique, which states that "both wish to reduce the danger of international military conflict" and "neither should seek hegemony in the Asia-Pacific region ...." One could certainly argue this way if taking the communique's provisions literally. Further contributing to this line of reasoning was the reduction by the U.S. of its military strength in the area at this juncture. Thus the actions of the People's Republic of China had undermined U.S.-China relations and the communiques upon which ties had been built (or at least one of them).[66]

The authors conclude in this chapter that the U.S. government "is responsible for holding up the settlement of the Taiwan question." The analysis they present in this chapter seems, in fact, to support this conclusion. On the other hand, one may doubt that the policy of the

---

64. That the possibility of the sale was announced in advance, to provoke debate or elicit support, seems to confirm the view that it was an effort to maintain a balance of power in the Taiwan Strait. See Daniel Sutherland, "Ban on F-16 Sales to Taiwan May End," *Washington Post*, September 2, 1992, p. A25.

65. Hickey, *United States-Taiwan Security Ties*, p. 81.

66. That U.S.-PRC relations were strained over Beijing's military build-up seems to have been reflected in Washington's decision to support Taipei's application to GATT, Ambassador James Lilley's statement that the PRC's views on unification were "outdated," and the same of F-16 fighter aircraft to the ROC. See Harry Harding, "America's China Dilemma," *The Annals*, January 1992, pp. 23-24 for further details.

People's Republic of China is really in contraposition to U.S. policy vis-a-vis Taiwan in most respects. Chinese leaders in Beijing have on numerous occasions stated that they will not renounce the use of force against Taiwan and have stated that they will launch an invasion of Taiwan or otherwise employ military force against the islands for certain reasons or under certain circumstances. This, one might say, is fundamental to Beijing's Taiwan policy. Never, however, have they mentioned any actions by the United States government as a cause for taking military action against Taiwan. This clearly appears to contradict their argument.

IV

The third chapter of this document is entitled "The Chinese Government's Basic Position Regarding Settlement of the Taiwan Question." The authors' starting point or fundamental assumption is that national unification is "a sacrosanct mission of the entire Chinese people." While such a statement may in some senses seem to be true, it is also hyperbole and may be thus regarded as propaganda. Since the People's Republic of China is not a democracy it is difficult to impossible to know the feelings or attitudes of its citizens. Observations of Western scholars and visitors who have been to the PRC seem to suggest that unification is generally viewed by the populace as a lofty goal and that it should be accomplished at some time in the future. Most, however, do not consider it an immediate or important objective. And many Chinese, especially young people and the politically active, seem to feel that until the People's Republic of China becomes democratic, Taiwan should remain separate because it best serves as a model for change in the PRC that way.[67] In Taiwan, while most of the population does not support separation, their position on unification varies from time to time. Clearly there is no support for unification as long as the mainland of China is ruled by a communist regime that is undemocratic and shows contempt for human rights. Thus, to say that unification is a sacrosanct mission of the entire Chinese population is obviously not a logical beginning premise.

---

67. Though it is difficult to discern how many people in the PRC hold this opinion, it has often been expressed by Chinese who call for democratic reform.

The authors then proceed to say that the People's Republic of China's basic position on the "Taiwan question" is peaceful reunification and that means realizing the "one country, two systems" model. They do not, however, follow up by suggesting how peaceful reunification and the "one country, two systems" formula are connected. They contend that the formula has its origins in the 1950s. But they do not mention the fact the U.S. proposed a peaceful solution agreement with PRC negotiators beginning in 1954 during their talks in Geneva and in subsequent discussions and received various replies, yet the "one country, two systems" formula was never mentioned.

They assert that this model or solution was formulated in the 1950s by Zhou Enlai (Chou En-lai) and Mao Zedong. In fact, they quote statements by Zhou in early 1955 and Mao in 1956 as proof. However, the phrase "one country, two systems" cannot be found in any statements by Mao or Zhou in the 1950s. Zhou's statements that are said to be the beginning of the "one country, two systems" policy are about two alternatives--war or peaceful means--to revolve the "Taiwan question." Zhou Enlai would probably have preferred a peaceful solution given what he said at other times on the subject.[68] But, his statements come just two months after the first Offshore Islands crisis, precipitated by a PRC attack on Nationalist-held islands off the coast of China. This was certainly not an auspicious context for Beijing to suggest a model for a peaceful solution to either the leaders or the population of the ROC. In fact, it seems inexplicable why the authors suggest that the "one country, two systems" formula was first broached in the 1950s.

In any case, what they aver is contradicted by what Chinese scholars have written and said about this matter. So say Chinese scholars, the term "one country, two systems" was first used, in connection with reunification, by Deng Xiaoping in 1978.[69] Deng, they

---

68. Of course, Zhou Enlai's more famous statement about Taiwan relates to the length of time the PRC could wait for reunification--suggesting a long time. Mao is also reported to have said in reference to the reunification question: "We can do without them for the time being, and let it come after 100 years." Cited in Henry Kissinger, *The White House Years* (Boston: Little, Brown and Company, 1979), p, 1062.

69. See J. Terry Emmerson, "An American View of One Country, Two Systems," *Issues and Studies*, September 1988, pp. 36-49 for further details. Also see Copper, *China Diplomacy*, pp. 81-87.

observe, said that Taiwan, after reunification, could retain its non-socialist economic system among other things.   However, he provided no elaboration about what this meant or how it might be reconciled with the fact that ROC possessed sovereignty, not to mention what the population of Taiwan or the international community might say about it.   In 1982, Deng used the phrase again in talks with Margaret Thatcher about the future of Hong Kong. This is when the concept became well known.   When, in fact, the phrase "one country, two systems" was given its current meaning or considered a model or formula for the reunification of Taiwan is difficult to say.

According to the document, the concept of "one country, two systems" also originated from the desires of overseas Chinese and people of Chinese descent to "join hands to work for a resurgence of China." The authors state: "It was against this historical background that the Chinese government formulated the position ...." Clearly this is an argument that defies common sense.   No one knows what people of Chinese blood think about this issue.   No polls have been taken. Scholars, in fact, until recently have not taken an interest in this matter.   Logic would say that there are many Chinese views on the subject of reunification.   Querying Overseas Chinese living in East or Southeast Asia certainly does not reveal a preoccupation with or support for "one country, two systems" or even an understanding of what it means.   Are we to believe that Mao or Zhou somehow (intuitively or by some mystical means) measured the global Chinese pulse on this issue?

In the next paragraph, the document refers to offers Beijing made to Taipei on January 1, 1979 at the time the United States de-recognized the Republic of China and established formal diplomatic ties with the People's Republic of China.   The problem evoked here is that any perceptive reader cannot help but wonder if the term was coined, or at least popularized, to pressure Taiwan at a time of crisis and at a time when it would have to negotiate from a position of weakness.   The government of the Republic of China at this time was suffering a severe credibility problem because of the withdrawal of diplomatic recognition by its most important friend and only superpower ally.   Are we then to conclude that the concept was first employed to bully and take advantage of Taipei?

Another difficulty engendered by bringing up the January 1979 proposal is that careful observers as well as probably a good portion of the population of Taiwan will recall that Beijing, at this time and later, made several offers in the form of numerical slogans: "three links," "four exchanges," and "nine principles." But these offers were not serious.[70] And many in Taiwan associated these with Maoist propaganda campaigns of the past. More important, Beijing made the proposals absent specifics about whether Taiwan was to be regarded as a province of China, as hard-liners had insisted, or whether it was to be a special municipality (like Shanghai and some other metropolitan areas in China--as Zhou Enlai had suggested), or whether it was to be an "autonomous region" like Tibet. In any event, all of these presented problems: the first because it was the hard-line position; the second because it didn't really say anything, except that Taiwan would be ruled by the State Council in Beijing; and the last because of what was widely known about the PRC's treatment of autonomous regions.

The document goes on to note that the late Chairman (of the National People's Congress) Ye Jianying (Yeh Chien-ying) further elaborated on the "policy and principles" relating to the one country, two systems formula in September 1981 in a proposal he made to Taiwan regarding unification. Ye's proposal contained nine points and thus it became known as the "Nine-Point Proposal." Among the points was a proposal for the free exchange of mail, trade visits and services. Observers wondered at the time if this was serious inasmuch as these things did not exist in the PRC at the time. Another was a promise by the PRC to help Taiwan financially. Since the ROC was by this time quite prosperous, with one of the largest foreign exchange positions in the world, and the PRC still a poor country, this was seen as a joke in Taiwan. In fact, to many people in Taiwan and in Western countries, the presence of this item among the nine points made the whole document seem less than serious. Still another point was that Taiwan would become a special administrative zone in the PRC.   This evoked fear and apprehension as people in Taiwan associated this with repression in Tibet and in other such regions in China.[71] Yet another provision in the proposal was that Taiwan investments in China would be guaranteed.   Looking back on this promise, Taiwan has invested

---

70. See Martin L. Lasater, *U.S. Interests in the New Taiwan* (Boulder: Westview Press, 1993), p. 112.

71. Ibid., pp. 112-14.

generously and with good results in terms of helping China grow economically; yet guarantees are still to be worked out.

Ye's offer, it must be understood, was preceded by efforts on the part of the People's Republic of China to isolate the ROC diplomatically and force Taipei to negotiate. It was thus taken, by the population in Taiwan, to be another attempt by Beijing to pressure Taiwan against its will (in terms of timing at least) to reunify. President Chiang Ching-kuo viewed it as an attempt to get the U.S. to stop arms sales to the ROC. Beijing had just downgraded its relations with Holland over arms sales to Taipei. Deng reportedly said not long after the proposal that the PRC may downgrade its relations with the United States.[72] It was definitely not seen as a change in policy or negotiating stance by Beijing. Perhaps also worth mentioning is that it was presaged by often-heard rumors to the effect that representatives of Beijing and Taipei were engaged in secret talks--rumors that seemed to originate from the People's Republic of China. In early 1981, Anna Chenault, wife of the former U.S. Air Force General Claire Chenault and an active member of the Republican Party, visited Deng Xiaoping. Then she went to Taipei and spoke to President Chiang Ching-kuo. This led some to believe that the "one country, two systems" idea was shrouded in secrecy and was not something to be discussed openly.[73]

Soon after the "nine-point" offer was made, the ROC's Premier Sun Yun-suan issued an official reply to Ye's offer. He said that China "could be unified on the basis of Sun Yat-sen's Three Principles of the People." After all, he said, Taiwan was obviously doing better than the other parts of China in both economic and political modernization and thus should serve as a model. His proposals were published by the ROC government.[74] This document received no attention in Beijing even though the PRC was at the time taking a new and different view of Sun Yat-sen and his writings. Moreover, the authors of the "White Paper"

---

72. See Ralph Clough, "The People's Republic of China and the Taiwan Relations Act," in Ramon H. Myers (ed.), *A Unique Relationship: The United States and the Republic of China under the Taiwan Relations Act* (Stanford: Hoover Institution Press, 1989), p. 127.

73. For details, see Copper, *China Diplomacy*, p. 79.

74. Sun Yun-suan, *The China Issue and China's Reunification* (Taipei: Government Information Office, 1982).

fail to mention Premier Sun's counterproposal or the document he penned.

The authors of the document refer to Deng citing the formula in 1981 and again in 1983 in connection with Taiwan's reunification. Then, they say, in 1992, General Secretary (of the Chinese Communist Party) Jiang Zemin spoke of talks between the Chinese Communist Party and the Nationalist Party, or Kuomintang. However, Jiang also included other parties, mass organizations and "all circles" on both sides that "could be invited." Apparently he realized that a proposal for party-to-party talks was not reasonable in view of the fact that the ROC no longer had a one-party system and that opposition groups, especially the Democratic Progressive Party (although Jiang did not refer to it by name), had to be allowed some input. Yet the DPP had spoken unequivocally in favor of separation. The DPP, as already noted, stated its opposition to reunification clearly and with great fanfare in what some called a "declaration of independence" before the 1991 election by making it a plank in the DPP's platform. Furthermore, Democratic Progressive Party leaders loudly registered complaints that they were deliberately left out of discussions about cross-strait relations. Did Jiang seek to give the DPP and other opponents of reunification a place in negotiations? This seemed implicit in his remarks; yet there was no follow-up. One also has to wonder if Beijing was willing to debate the issue of independence or not. Another question might be asked: Did Beijing's negotiating stance change during this period? The authors are talking about a considerable period of time. Finally, one might question why PRC policy makers failed to recognize or even take cognizance of counter-proposals by Taipei. In March 1989, a legislator in Taipei coined the term "one country, two equal governments." This phrase subsequently became very popular in Taiwan and was mentioned often by scholars and the press.[75] In May, Premier Hau said this was the ROC's position.[76] In September 1990, the Executive Yuan in its semi-annual report to the Legislative Yuan, used the term "one country, two areas"--which had come into popular use to the point some call it official policy.

---

75. Clough, *Bridging the Taiwan Strait* (Boulder, CO: Westview Press, 1993), p. 16.

76. Ibid., p. 131.

In any event, the PRC's proposals to implement the "one country, two systems" formula failed to become credible or even well known as a means of dealing with Taipei. Instead, the formula became well known only when cited in the context of negotiations between the People's Republic of China and the U.K. regarding Hong Kong and when an agreement was reached in September 1984 whereby Hong Kong would be returned to the PRC in July 1997. Provision was made for Hong Kong to retain its capitalist economic and social system for fifty years (Deng Xiaoping later promised one hundred years). Hong Kong was to be essentially self-governing through locally-elected officials and there would be a separation of powers and checks and balances, or at least this was suggested. Also, the People's Liberation Army was not to be stationed in Hong Kong. Finally, the Universal Declaration on Human Rights would remain in effect and Hong Kong would retain the right to belong to and participate in international organizations and send trade missions abroad. Hong Kong was to be labelled a "Special Administrative Region" after reunification.[77]

The U.K., it must be pointed out, was not in such a bargaining position to extract any meaningful concessions from the PRC regarding Hong Kong's future. Hong Kong was a colony when the days of colonies had passed. And Hong Kong was difficult if not impossible to defend militarily and was not self-sufficient economically. Thus, Beijing dictated the terms, many of which were couched in vague language, making it easy to find loopholes or excuses not to fulfill the agreement. In any case, the PRC subsequently flouted and violated many of its provisions and Britain could do little in response save issue a few complaints and protests. Thus few observers in Taiwan or elsewhere feel that the PRC's negotiating stance on Hong Kong, in terms of it setting a precedent that Taiwan might wish to follow, was auspicious.[78] The same may be said about what happened in ensuing

---

77. See *A Draft Agreement between the Government of the United Kingdom of Great Britain and Northern Ireland and the Government of the People's Republic of China on the Future of Hong Kong* (London: Her Majesty's Government, September 26, 1994).

78. See Brian S.Y. Weng, "Taiwan and Hong Kong, 1987: A Review," in Anthony G. Kane (ed.), *China Briefing, 1988* (Boulder: Westview Press, 1988). It is also worth noting in this connection that the "Basic Law" on Hong Kong Special Administrative Region was promulgated in April 1990, less than a year after the

years. Many people have fled Hong Kong to take up residence elsewhere or obtain passports or residency permits and return to Hong Kong with "insurance" so they can leave in 1997 if Beijing does not live up to its promises.[79]

Because the ROC is not a colony, but rather is a sovereign nation-state, and can be defended militarily, not to mention a host of other reasons why it is not like Hong Kong, Hong Kong seldom viewed as a model for reunification that applies to Taiwan. In fact, most in Taiwan view Beijing's suggestion that Hong Kong's reunification can serve as a prototype for Taiwan's "returning to the motherland" as somewhere between meaningless and absurd.[80]

The authors go on to argue what they call the "basic contents" of the "one country, two systems" idea. They relate it to "building socialism with Chinese characteristics" and say that it is a "fundamental state policy of the Chinese government that will not change for a long time to come." Why it is related to "building socialism with Chinese characteristics"--which is not well defined in the eyes of most scholars (and is perhaps an oxymoron in view of the capitalist nature of the Chinese people)--is uncertain. At any rate they proceed quickly from there to other arguments.

Their next point is that there is only one China and that Taiwan is an inalienable part of China. They say this is a "universally accepted fact as well as the premise for a peaceful settlement of the Taiwan question." There is considerable evidence, however, to suggest that it is not a universally recognized fact. There are now twenty-nine nations in the world that have official or formal diplomatic ties with the Republic of China. Moreover, it is widely thought that this number would be higher if Taipei wanted to pursue establishing relations with more nations, which it apparently does not in order to preserve

Tiananmen Massacre and did not reflect the spirit of promises made earlier.

79. About 45,000 people left Hong Kong annually in the late 1980s, double the rate of 1984. In 1991 it had increased to 55,000 to 60,000. See Parris H. Chang, "China's Relations with Hong Kong and Taiwan," *The Annals*, January 1992, p. 133. The author notes that people in Taiwan watched with considerable apprehension what was happening in Hong Kong.

80. See Yu-ming Shaw, "Taiwan: A View from Taipei," *Foreign Affairs*, Summer 1985, pp. 1050-63, and Yu-ming Shaw, "An ROC View of the Hong Kong Issue," *Issues and Studies*, January 1986, p. 30.

amicable relations with the People's Republic of China.[81] Their argument is also discredited by the fact that many nations, when they established diplomatic ties with the People's Republic of China only "took note" of Beijing's claim over Taiwan; they did not support it.[82] Finally, the Republic of China has what can be called informal or pseudo-diplomatic relations with many countries of the world. And these ties are being upgraded. Various nations have given their offices in Taipei more formal sounding names; others have sent political leaders of note to Taipei. Finally, a sizeable number have received Taipei's leaders in formal or official fashion.[83]

---

81. It is known in Taiwan and in diplomatic circles elsewhere that there are a number of countries that have expressed an interest in establishing formal diplomatic ties with the ROC. The number is said to range from five to over twenty. Most appear to be seeking economic assistance from Taipei.

82. Actually there has been a variety of responses from members of the international community to the PRC's claim to Taiwan when establishing diplomatic ties with Beijing. Some recognized the PRC as the sole government representing the Chinese people and that Taiwan is an indispensable part of the territory of the PRC. Others agreed to the first part but did not mention Taiwan. Some only acknowledged Beijing's position. Still other merely "took note." Finally some stated they "fully understood and respect" Beijing's position. For further details, see Vernon V. Aspaturian," International Reactions and Responses to the PRC's Use of force against Taiwan," in Parris H. Chang and Martin Lasater (eds.), *If China Crosses the Taiwan Strait: The International Response*, (Lanham, MD: University Press of America, 1993), p. 126.

83. The Republic of China had, as of late 1993, ninety representative offices abroad in sixty countries with which it had no formal diplomatic ties. Seventeen of these used the Republic of China in its name. Thirty seven countries with which Taipei had no diplomatic links had set up offices of some kind in Taipei to issue visas. For further details, see *The Republic of China Yearbook 1994* (Taipei: Government Information Office, 1993), p. 174. This compares to unofficial ties with thirty countries and representative offices in 55 countries in 1991. See report by Foreign Minister Frederick Chien to KMT Central Standing Committee, January 8, 1992, *Chung Yang Jih Pao*, January 10, 1992 cited in FBIS January 17, 1992, p. 55. In short, the ROC has made considerable progress in its conduct of informal diplomacy in recent years.

A second point to support the one-China position is that "Chinese people on both sides of the Straits [sic] all believe that there is only one China and espouse reunification." On the contrary, a small though perhaps significant number in Taiwan, as reflected in public opinion surveys over the years, have recorded views that would be defined by anyone reading the polls as supporting independence.[84] Many more support separation in the short-term. Worthy of note in this connection is the number supporting separation or independence increases or decreases depending upon the policies and actions of Beijing. For example, it increased after the Tiananmen Massacre in June 1989. It increased following the Thousand Islands Lake incident in March 1994 when twenty-four tourists from Taiwan were murdered in the People's Republic of China, after which the PRC government at first denied that it had happened and then executed accused soldiers with little or no due process and so quickly that a coverup seemed evident.[85]

Further evidence that not everyone in Taiwan espouses unification, at least at the present time, are polls indicating that the population of the Republic of China supports the government's policies, particularly its foreign policies, by a significant majority.[86] Since the government's policy on unification may be said to be unification in the future but not now, or maintaining the *status quo*, a large majority of the people of Taiwan, by supporting the government, seem to espouse the same view-- one that is clearly not an unequivocal view in support of unification. The ROC government also takes the position that reunification is contingent on the People's Republic of China experiencing further political development and economic integration. The population of Taiwan seems to support this view as well.

---

84. This question has been asked in public opinion polls many times over the years. See, for example, Liao Kuang-sheng, "China's State Structure and National Unification," in Kuan and Brosseau, *China Review* (Hong Kong: Chinese University Press, 1991), p. 4.11.

85. See various issues of newspapers published in Taiwan during April and May 1994 for polls indicating a drop in the positive responses given by citizens when asked about the PRC or about unification versus independence.

86. In 1990, the government's public approval rating was 50.5 percent on foreign policy. The disapproval rate was very low. See Lasater, *U.S. Interests in the New Taiwan*, p. 60.

The second point the authors make is that "socialism on the mainland and capitalism on Taiwan can coexist." While it is not difficult to imagine that the two can coexist, it seems another matter for the ROC and the PRC to unify as long as they have incompatible economic systems and different social and political systems that are in large part an outgrowth of their respective economic systems. The People's Republic of China has been moving in the direction of capitalism (some say this is what "socialism with Chinese characteristics" means) and seems to have already gone very far in this direction (with a larger percentage of production in the private sector than some Western European countries). Nevertheless, capitalism may still be fragile in China as indicated by the many setbacks and reversals to Deng's reforms since 1978. Economic ties being the strongest force bringing the two sides together, one could argue that it will take further progress in the People's Republic of China in the direction of capitalism and free markets and even more extensive economic ties across the Taiwan Strait before there will be strong sentiments in support of unification in Taiwan.

Third, the authors say that Taiwan, after reunification, will become a "special administrative region" and will have a "high degree of autonomy." The main difficulty with such a proposal is the bad record of communist rule in the People's Republic of China's autonomous regions. The case of jitters in Hong Kong caused by the prospect of this has already been cited. Tibet is another case in point; in fact, it is a much more instructive case in the negative sense. It is the poorest part of China and is an area where human rights abuses abound. This is well documented and is an embarrassment to the PRC whenever it is mentioned. The same situation obtains to a somewhat lesser extent in China's other "autonomous regions." In short, these "regions" have been misruled and mistreated by the government of the People's Republic of China.[87]

The proposal then that Taiwan should become a special administrative zone is an ominous one. To the population of Taiwan, or, for that matter any astute observer, the use of the term "autonomous

---

87. For details, see June Teufel Dreyer, *China's Forty Millions: Minority Nationalities and Integration in the People's Republic of China* (Cambridge, MA: *Harvard University Press, 1976)* and *June Teufel Dreyer*, China's Political System: Modernization and Tradition (New York: Paragon House, 1993), chapter 13.

region" conjures up thoughts of mismanagement, ill treatment, forced relocation of large numbers of people, massive human rights abuses, economic stagnation, etc. It was certainly a bad choice of words. Also, if the authors' proposals are to be believed, one must wonder why, assuming Taipei probably will not bring the territory under its sovereignty into an alliance with another country and is "building bridges" to the PRC, maintaining the *status quo* (meaning Taipei keeping its sovereignty) is not a good option. This would seem particularly so in view relations between Beijing and Taipei having improved markedly over the last ten-plus years and for the most part seem to be quite cordial now, not to mention the loss of face and prestige and the foreign criticism that would inevitably follow Beijing's incorporation of Taiwan if there were any sign of misgovernance. That would surely be the case if incorporation were to occur by force or through pressure.

Fourth, the authors favor "peace negotiations" between the two parties on "any subject" and about which "groups or personalities" may participate in said talks. This seems reasonable and generous. This would be especially so if the parties mentioned could include the ROC government and there could be government-to-government talks--which is the usual mode of negotiating to resolve matters that may lead to conflict or war. Unfortunately the negotiating position of Beijing has excluded government-to-government talks. Thus, the best and the usual way of resolving differences in international politics cannot be employed.

The authors call for "mutual respect, complementary and mutual benefit ... direct trade, postal, air and shipping services ...." This is quite reasonable. But in the next paragraph they say that Beijing may use military force to resolve questions. Thus they seem to contradict their reasonable proposals and undermine their efforts to establish confidence in the government and the population of the ROC, which is necessary for negotiations to proceed and accomplish anything.[88]

In this context, they reject any analogy to the cases of Germany and Korea, saying that these divided nations were the result of "international accords at the end of the Second World War." Why this

---

88. The fact that the government of North Korea, regarded by many as an outlaw or aggressive regime, has signed a non-aggression pact with South Korea, in particular makes the PRC appear unreasonable.

matters is not clear. They then go on to state that the Chinese government "has always opposed applying the German or Korean formulas to Taiwan." Since the ROC is generally regarded to possess sovereignty, which makes the situation similar to the two Germanys before unification and the two Koreas now (pending unification), and the fact that any solution that might work peacefully should be acceptable (for discussion at least), one has to question if this a wise policy. The unabashed efforts by the PRC to isolate Taiwan is a policy that is plainly not in accord with a new world order that eschews isolating any nation, people or political entity and favors "universal" (meaning membership is open to all nations and in some cases other political actors) regional and international organizations.

V

Chapter IV of the document speaks of the "present division between the two sides of the Taiwan Straits [sic]" as a "misfortune for the Chinese nation." To resolve it, the authors declare, the government of the People's Republic of China has made proposals and has adopted measures to "step up the development of inter-Straits [sic] relations." They speak of measures taken in three categories: political, military and economic.

In the political realm, the authors make mention of the Supreme People's Court and the Supreme People's Procuratorate having decided to no longer prosecute people who have gone to Taiwan for offenses committed prior to the founding of the People's Republic. While this is certainly to be considered a friendly gesture, it must be regarded as that, a gesture, since the offenses under question involve things that happened forty-five years or more ago. Most of the people that might otherwise be prosecuted are dead or are very old. The overwhelming majority of the crimes are either political in nature or were committed during wartime or in the conduct of military activities. Moreover, most of these "crimes" would not be prosecuted by other governments and many of these crimes appear to have been committed with justification, meaning that in the judicial systems of democratic countries or in the court of world opinion there would probably be no trial and little hope for a conviction.

Dr. Han Lih-wu is a case in point. Dr. Han died in 1991. He was reportedly the last person on the "most-wanted" list in the People's

Republic of China at the time he died. The crimes which made him a "most wanted" person involved shipping China's natural treasures, antiques and artifacts of various kinds, to Taiwan in 1949. These treasures were carefully protected by Dr. Han when he was in China and after he arrived in Taiwan. In 1965 they were put on display in the Palace Museum near Taipei--regarded by many who have seen it as the most magnificent museum in the world. Should these treasures be in Beijing instead? This is a moot question since most would have been destroyed, stolen, sold or otherwise lost during the civil war had not Dr. Han made the efforts he did to save them. The Communist Party and the Red Army at this time sought to extinguish "the old" and build a "New China." Antiques, old books and historical objects were purposely destroyed. Had they not been "lost" at this time it is very probable that they would have been later during the Great Proletarian Cultural Revolution, when rampaging Red Guards sought to smash or wipe out anything that represented "old China," capitalist or bourgeoisie culture, or anything that made anyone not fit the mold of Mao's egalitarian utopia. Precious antiques and artifacts and art were destroyed *en mass* e at this time. Clearly China is better for what Dr. Han did. Yet he was made a wanted man for this.[89]

The authors then proceed to discuss other categories of problems, omitting any discussion of the real political issues that pose a barrier to better relations across the Taiwan Strait. The biggest impediment to better relations between Taipei and Beijing is manifestly the unwillingness of the People's Republic of China to recognize the legitimacy of the government of the Republic of China. The second is Beijing's unwillingness to accept a peaceful solution to resolve their problems and stop talking of using military force to resolve the "Taiwan issue." PRC leaders, in this connection, argue that Taiwan's future is a domestic matter even though Beijing does not govern Taiwan and never has.

The people of Taiwan realize this as does their government. So does the international community. The PRC's position is, therefore, neither a persuasive nor a friendly one. Moreover, regarding the threat of force, Beijing is in violation of the United Nations Charter. One of the seven principles of the U.N. is the duty of members to settle

---

89. For details on this, see P. Van DeMeerssche, *A Life to Treasure* (London: The Sherwood Press, 1987). This book is a biography of Dr. Han.

disputes by peaceful means. This principle has also become a part of general or customary international law.[90]   Though it may be argued that this is a frequent violation in the world today, it is nevertheless unlawful and it is not taken lightly in Taiwan.

In short, what the PRC has failed to do, if one assumes that it truly wants to lower tensions in the Taiwan Strait area and foster better relations between Beijing and Taipei, is what is often called confidence building. Taipei cannot be expected to enter into serious negotiations on issues that remain unresolved until some trust has been established. By considering the government of the Republic of China an illegitimate regime, Beijing has not fostered confidence amokng the people or with negotiators Taiwan. It has done just the opposite. The same goes for its refusal to accept a peaceful solution and its continued threats of invasion or other military action against Taiwan. That being the case, PRC leaders should expect Taipei to bristle and refuse to talk. Similarly, they should not anticipate that Taiwan will shift away from policies that have been created by unfriendly acts on Beijing's part in the past without some actions that would warrant this.

Finding common ground for talks is also a problem. Or put another way, there needs to be a framework for talks. The authors of this document reject the German and Korea formulas for resolution of the Taiwan issue. They do this because they do not want to give credence or support to the Republic of China's claim to sovereignty. They appear to be oblivious of the fact that East and West Germany, by permitting dual recognition, which allowed both to have extensive diplomatic ties with nations of the world and join the United Nations, produced the confidence and trust (in the case of the two Germanys) required of both sides for serious negotiations that led to unification. While Korea is, of course, a different situation, many feel that negotiations founded on both North Korea and South Korea recognizing the sovereignty and legitimacy of the other (which before 1991 North Korea refused to do) and both joining the United Nations will pave the way for unification talks there.

A number of scholars, in fact, take the German model for the reunification very seriously. The German example, according to one analyst, presents a very useful precedent:

---

90. See Robert L. Bledsoe and Boleslaw A. Boczek, *The International Law Dictionary* (Santa Barbara: ABC-CLIO Press, 1987), p. 308.

Germany seems an apt model for current relations between the
ROC and the PRC because it has witnessed several different
types of unification and separation that are relevant for the
current situation in China and which encompass the possible
process and outcomes in the Taiwan Strait area. First, the
creation of Germany in the late nineteenth century represents a
dramatic case of national unification and integration. In
contrast, the *Anschluss* with [of] Austria in 1938 in essence
represented a military conquest that proved unstable in the
sense that Austria became an independent and sovereign
"German" nation-state following the defeat of Nazi Germany
in World War II. Finally, the recent reunification of East and
West Germany in 1990 proves the possibility of almost
instantaneously merging societies divided by the Cold War
under the right political and international conditions.[91]

Not only does the People's Republic of China reject the German
formula for reunification, a formula that has worked, but Beijing does
not offer another formula that has a track record. It rather, or only,
suggests the "one country, two systems" formula that has been discussed
earlier. Obviously it needs to devise a better proposal. Others have
suggested additional formulas, but Beijing has rejected these also.[92]

---

91. Cal Clark and Steve Chan, "ROC-PRC (Non) Relations: Groping Toward the
German Model," in Bih-jaw Lin and James T. Myers (eds.), *Forces for Change in
Contemporary China* (Taipei: Institute of International Relations, 1992), p. 348.

92. Parris Chang, formerly a professor of political science at Pennsylvania State
University and now a member of the Legislative Yuan representing the Democratic
Progressive Party in Taiwan, has suggested the Singapore model. He suggests that
the KMT drop its claims to China and not challenge the legitimacy of the PRC
government and co-exist as two nations. Chang and a number of other scholars
have suggested the commonwealth model, a loose association of two independent
states. Fei Xiping, also a noted politician in Taiwan, has suggested a
confederation, which would link the PRC and ROC by a non-binding treaty, yet
would allow both autonomy in both domestic and foreign affairs. Wei Yung,
another member of the Legislative Yuan, has promoted the "multi-state model"—
which is similar to the Germany formula.   For details, see Liao Kuang-sheng,
"China's State Structure and National Unification," in Kuan Hsin-chi and

Meanwhile, the PRC continues to try to isolate the Republic of China and undermine or destroy its diplomatic ties with other countries, as witnessed by continued efforts on Beijing's part to reduce the number of nations with which Taipei has official diplomatic contacts, the number and significance of its unofficial ties and its contacts with international political organizations. Beijing is even so petty as to object to the U.N. and other international government organizations publishing economic and other statistics on Taiwan. This cannot be seen as confidence building.

Richard Nixon, who may have been considered China's best friend in the West until his death recently, made the following comment: "A more prosperous Taiwan serves China's interests. A more prosperous China serves Taiwan's interests. Beijing should drop its opposition to Taiwan's membership in international organizations."[93] Clearly Beijing would be well advised to listen to this.

The document goes on to say that "initiatives have been taken to ease military confrontations across the Straits [sic]". As proof, mention is made of discontinuing the shelling of Kinmen (Quemoy) and other nearby islands. In addition, "forward defense positions" have been "transformed into economic development zones or tourist attractions."

The fact that the PRC has stopped bombing Kinmen and other islands is not of great significance. Chinese leaders, after the second Offshore Islands crisis in 1958 said they did not plan to attack the islands again apart from a full-scale invasion of Taiwan.[94] If what they say is to be believed then stopping the bombardment of the islands is meaningless, or perhaps even an ominous sign. Furthermore, since the bombardment ended fourteen years before this document was written, it cannot be considered a recent event of significance.[95]

Maurice Brosseau (eds.), *China Review*, pp. 4.12-4.13.

93. Richard M. Nixon, *Beyond Peace* (New York: Random House, 1994), p. 134.

94. Ralph Clough, *Reaching Across the Taiwan Strait*, p. 9.

95. It is also worthy of note that the Standing Committee of the National People's Congress, at this time, i.e. 1979, said that it would "take present realities into account and respect the *status quo* ... and the opinions of people in all walks of life and adopt reasonable policies and measures ...." The PRC also stopped using the term "liberation" of Taiwan and spoke instead of "peaceful reunification." More recently, however, Beijing's language toward Taiwan has not been so soft or

The "transforming" of forward positions, similarly, cannot be seen as significant--but for much different reasons. This action on the PRC's part is much more than offset, in fact, many, many fold, by its general military buildup, which has been huge in the past five years. Other nations in the region have seen it as threatening and destabilizing. It has been, according to a variety of other analysts, somewhere in the range of 100 to one 150 percent since 1988.[96] In 1992 alone, the PRC bought $U.S. 1.5 billion in weapons from Moscow.[97] And this happened at a time when PRC leaders described their security situation in terms of external threats as the best it has been in years.[98] What is more, the People's Republic of China has been able to withdraw forces from the Sino-Soviet border because of reduced tension there. Some of these forces have been placed closer to the Taiwan Strait, an action viewed in Taipei with apprehension. Making matters worse, Beijing has listed the Taiwan Strait as a likely site of military action.[99] Finally, mention must be made that the PRC has purchased new aircraft and has been expanding its naval power, giving it greater naval capabilities as well that directly threaten Taiwan.[100]

Clearly, Taiwan cannot feel more secure with the arrival of a new world order due to what the People's Republic of China has done to upgrade and strengthen its military in recent years. Rather, the ROC

---

conciliatory. For details on the pronouncements in 1979, see Robert L. Downen, *To Bridge the Taiwan Strait* (Washington: Council for Social and Political Studies, 1984), pp. 104-7.

96. See Nicholas D. Kristof, "China Raises Military Budget Despite Deficit," *New York Times*, March 17, 1993, p. A7.

97. Larry M. Wortzel, "China Pursues Traditional Great Power Status," *Orbis*, Spring 1994, p. 165.

98. See *People's Daily*, Dec. 18, 1992 for details.

99. Ross H. Monroe, "Eavesdropping on the Chinese Military: Where it Expects War--Where it Doesn't, *Orbis*, Summer 1994, pp. 317-58.

100. See Michael D. Swaine, "The Modernization of the Chinese People's Liberation Army: Prospects and Implications for Northeast Asia," *Analysis* (National Bureau of Asian Research), Vol. 5, No. 3, October 1994 and Lee Kuan Yew on China-Taiwan Reunification," *Straits Times*, January 30, 1993, cited in *FBIS* (East Asia), Feb 3, 1993, pp 36-37.

has had to take drastic measures to maintain its security in the face of changes in the balance of forces in the Taiwan Strait area.[101]

Next the authors of the document cite progress on the "economic plane." They note that "doors have been flung open." Indeed they have been and this has had a vast impact on cross-Strait relations. However, some caveats need to be made about this progress.

If one makes a general statement about the trends affecting Taiwan's unification with China or its separation or independence, it might be this: Politically, the ROC is going its own way; there is little or no convergence, so to speak, with the PRC. Economically it is integrating with the mainland, or the People's Republic of China. These are contradictory trends and it is difficult to say which will prevail. However, it may be relevant to note the following: If the new world order is based on economic power and commercial or trade blocs are forming, the PRC and the ROC, are probably going to be in the same bloc--either a Pacific Rim bloc led by Japan or a "Greater China" bloc or sub-bloc led by Beijing. It is worthy of note in this connection that many observers of international affairs perceive the rise of "Greater China" as a global trend of great salience, along with the demise of communism, a global economy, regionalism, etc.[102] There are, of course, some alternatives wherein the two China's are not bloc partners, but these scenarios seem rather remote at this juncture.

Hence, economic cooperation appears to be the key to unification, if unification is going to happen. Some facts regarding the growing economic links across the Taiwan Strait are, hence, instructive. Trade between the two players across the Taiwan Strait has increased very rapidly in recent years. ROC exports to the mainland or the PRC have grown by a phenomenal 20 percent per month for the last three years.[103]

---

101. In addition to purchasing F-16 fighter planes, Taipei has also bought French-made Mirage planes and is producing its own fighter plane called the IDF or Indigenous Defense Fighter. And it has purchased defensive missiles and other weapons. The ROC's defense buildup is considered necessary by the population and has strong public support.

102. See David Shambough, "Introduction: The Emergence of Greater China," *China Quaterly*, December 1993, p. 653.

103. Julian Baum, "A Different Age," *Far Eastern Economic Review*, June 30, 1994, p. 56.

Total trade volume is officially reported to have exceeded $U.S. 8 billion in 1993, and was probably considerably higher than this, or between $U.S. 10 and $U.S. 15 billion. Some put the figure at $U.S. 20 billion for 1994.[104] It is estimated that the ROC exported almost $U.S. 9 billion in goods to the PRC in the first six months of 1994, an increase of over 10.5 percent. PRC exports to the ROC have also been increasing.[105] In 1994, the PRC, or the mainland, became Taiwan's largest trading partner.

The PRC, ROC and Hong Kong ranked, respectively, the eleventh, thirteenth and eighth leading trading powers in the world in 1993. Trade among them amounted to $U.S. 636 billion--or 8.5 percent of the total exchange of goods in the world.[106] Andthis "group" trade is increasing at a rapid pace. Clearly the three constitute an economic bloc that can challenge the European Community, the North American Free Trade Association and Japan, if necessary. The Asian Development Bank recently noted that the PRC, ROC and Hong Kong have averaged 8.2 percent annual gross national product growth and this has made other Asian countries depend on this Greater China "de facto zone."[107]

Investment too has reached a very significant level. In 1989, it was estimated that Taiwan investors put $U.S. 1 billion in the PRC, which, at the time, was 9 percent of the total investment received by China. By the end of 1991, officially the total figure was $U.S. 3 billion.[108] In 1992 and 1993, it increased to the point that, according to PRC figures, it

---

104. Julian Baum, "Ready When You Are," *Far Eastern Economic Review*, September 15, 1994, p. 62.

105. See "Trade with mainland grows," *Free China Journal*, September 2, 1994, p. 3.

106. Allen Pun, "'Greater China, intriguing but elusive," *Free China Journal*, July 1, 1994, p. 7.

107. See Asian Development Bank's 1993 yearbook, cited in Ibid. It is worthy of note in this connection that the world economy grew by only 1.1 percent in 1993 according to the Wharton School. See Deborah Shen, "Brighter forecast for economy," *Free China Journal*, August 29, 1994, p. 3.

108. Parris H. Chang, "Beijing's Relations with Taiwan," in Parris H. Chang and Martin L. Lasater (eds.), *If China Crosses the Taiwan Strait: The International Response*, p. 8.

totalled $U.S. 19 billion by the end of 1993 and helped finance twenty-one thousand companies or enterprises.[109] The ROC is now easily the PRC's leading source of investment capital from any "nation" (though still behind Hong Kong). One could not have imagined this a decade ago. It reflects growing economic ties across the Taiwan Strait, which must be seen as no less than spectacular in almost any context. Clearly, this, in addition to trade across the Strait, is integrating the PRC and ROC economies. This has and will continue to lead, unless political difficulties arise, to a crumbling of barriers and the building of better relations between Beijing and Taipei.

However, to think economic interaction and mutual inter-dependence (which has obviously been created by trade and investment) will continue to increase, one must make some assumptions. Increased economic ties will certainly be contingent upon the PRC continuing its drive toward free market capitalism. The authors have spoken of merging Taiwan's capitalist economy with China's socialist economy. Is this really a meaningful idea? In many respects, the PRC's economy is no longer socialist and that is precisely why economic ties across the Taiwan Strait have grown so fast in recent years. Still Beijing must continue privatizing state-owned industries while making its economic system even more open and capitalist if it is to build economic links with the ROC. It must resolve the contradiction of a capitalist economic system and a communist political system. It must cope with centrifugal or secessionist tendencies. It must continue to allow foreign influence in China, including Western and Overseas Chinese as well as ROC influence. It must develop a legal system that is conducive to the further development of a market economy.[110] It must allow the free flow of information to ensure continued economic maturation. And, finally, it will have to democratize.

All of these things depend on Beijing, not Taipei. Thus the ball is in the court of the continental side of the Taiwan Strait, so to speak, not the island side. The authors talk as if Taipei must continue to cooperate to make economic cooperation work. However, it is

---

109. Sofia Wu, "U.S. 19 billion poured into mainland," *China Post* (International Edition), August 20, 1994, p. 3.

110. Margaret Thatcher mentions these things as conditions for increasing meaningful ties across the Taiwan Strait in a speech she gave in Taipei in August 1992. See "The Future has no Borders," *Free China Review*, p. 35.

transparent to most observers that future economic cooperation depends more on Beijing. Taiwan's economy is already a free and open one. The ROC is already a part of the global, capitalist economic system; the PRC is not.

This is not to say that there are no problems for the ROC in expanding economic contacts. Given Beijing's use and manipulation of trade and economic ties in the past, the ROC government is reluctant to become too dependent upon the "China market" or allow too large a portion of its trade to be with one country. Many in Taiwan fear more extensive economic ties for other reasons. In fact, Taipei has adopted what is called a "southern strategy"--encouraging more trade and investment with Southeast Asia instead of the mainland--in response to these fears.[111]   Beijing must, therefore, continue to change its economic system and build trust in Taiwan about further economic integration if economic ties are to increase appreciably beyond the present level. The PRC must also be willing to sell raw materials to the ROC and to jointly resolve disputes over oil and other mineral rights in the area.   In fact, there are a number of other questions that must be worked out, not the least of which is the creation of a legal framework to protect ROC citizens when they visit the PRC and their investments and property there.

Clearly, if the PRC wants trade and investment and other economic ties to further increase across the Taiwan Strait, it faces an impasse, or at least limitations, in continuing to regard the ROC as a renegade province of China and its government an illegal one. The same may be said about its unwillingness to foreswear the use of military force against Taiwan and its frequent threats and bellicose statements toward the ROC.

VI

The fifth section of this document is entitled "Several Questions Involving Taiwan in International Relations." Here the authors take up several special issues or problems relating to Taiwan's participation in global affairs and express their opposition to the ROC being a participant in international politics.

---

111. For further details, see *Republic of China Yearbook 1994*, p. 203

They begin with the premise that the "Government of the People's Republic of China has been recognized by the United Nations and throughout the world as the sole legal government representing the entire Chinese people." Inasmuch as twenty-nine governments accord official diplomatic recognition to the Republic of China, as noted earlier, this statement is obviously false. The government of the PRC, therefore, clearly has not been recognized "throughout the world" as the sole legal government representing the Chinese people. That is unless the population of Taiwan is regarded by the authors as not being Chinese, but rather as Taiwanese, as some advocates of independence suggest.

Also, contrary to what the authors opine, the Republic of China is generally seen as a legally constituted "Chinese" government. It is often called just Taiwan, rather than the Republic of China, but this does not appreciably affect the argument. Clearly the ROC is a legal political authority ruling Chinese people. And, if one considers Taipei's increasing diplomatic contacts, the upgrading of its mission abroad, etc., one has to conclude that the ROC is more and more being seen as another Chinese government or at least one that is retaining its sovereignty.

And it is not the only one. The case of Singapore is worth citing in this context. The population of Singapore is approximately 80 percent Chinese. Mandarin Chinese is an official language in Singapore, as in the PRC. Singapore is culturally Chinese. Almost all of its top leaders have been and are Chinese. Thus one may think of Singapore as a "Chinese nation-state."

In fact, Singapore is both a Chinese nation and a nation-state with undenied sovereignty. Singapore is recognized diplomatically by most nations in the world. It has embassies in capitals all over the world. Singapore is a member of the United Nations and most other governmental international organizations not to mention non-governmental international organizations.

If the PRC regards itself as the "sole legal government representing the entire Chinese people," why does it not object to Singapore's status in the world? Why does it object only to the ROC? One can offer a number of explanations: China's claim to Taiwan has historical roots. The PRC fought bitterly against the Nationalists for a number of years in the past. Many on both sides still think of the other as the enemy. During the Cold War, the Republic of China represented China in the world community and in various international organizations--including the United Nations until 1971. Chinese leaders in Beijing resented this; many perhaps still do. The ROC is still a competing regime. In short, recent history explains Beijing's policy of regarding Taiwan as its property and the object of incorporation rather than its claim to be the only Chinese government in the world.

Yet this doesn't necessarily seem to be at issue. At least Beijing has not mentioned these things much in recent years. While the two regimes or governments were once at war, and, of course it is possible they may be once again, most Chinese leaders appear to have laid to rest contentious issues of recent history. They apparently realize that historical problems don't play the role in international relations they once did, or, for that matter, in relations across the Taiwan Strait. Likewise, most PRC leaders don't seem to be bothered that much by past events, or at least they say this in making overtures to Taipei and/or the population of Taiwan. Otherwise why would its leaders make peaceful gestures toward Taiwan and express a desire for non-military means for resolving their problems?

Nor does Beijing seem object that much to Taiwan's representation of Chinese elsewhere. For example, when the elected bodies of government in Taiwan were recently reconstituted by Constitutional amendment, the PRC did not protest the inclusion of Overseas Chinese representation. In fact, they approved it. They no doubt did so because not doing this would have made the separation between the two Chinas, or China and Taiwan, greater. Rational minds prevailed.

It seems then that the policy in question, namely that the PRC is the only legal Chinese government, stated in the "White Paper" has two possible origins.

One, it resulted from making a concession to hard-liners in the top leadership or was put into the document by them, without thinking about its logic or consistency. Back to this point below.

Two, most PRC leaders see no hope of persuading Singapore (either its government or its population) to become part of the People's Republic of China and see no support for such a proposal in the international community. Conversely, they do see some hope of incorporating Taiwan by pressuring other countries with whom Beijing has diplomatic ties and by using Beijing's position of strength in the U.N. (its right to use the veto as a permanent member of the Security

Council). This is power politics--which, ironically, the PRC has long condemned.

But one must assume that if Taiwan is regarded as PRC property and Singapore is not, then PRC leaders, if the writers of this document represent them, are thinking of reunification by political or military means, not through economic integration. This seems odd given the powerful economic forces that now attract all Chinese political entities to the PRC, not to mention the Overseas Chinese living in Southeast Asia and elsewhere. Are PRC leaders ignoring the economic forces at work? That seems hard to believe, yet this seems to be what the authors are suggesting.

In connection with the argument being pursued, it should similarly be noted that the People's Republic of China has in the past espoused a legal position regarding its subjects called *jus sanguinis*--or Chinese subject by blood. Based on this concept the PRC has claimed the allegiance of Overseas Chinese or Chinese people living elsewhere. While it still technically adheres to this concept, it has taken actions and made statements indicating it does not claim Chinese elsewhere as its citizens.[112] Given this change in *de facto* policy one might conclude that Beijing has changed its position regarding its right to claim and to represent Chinese "throughout the world." Might it change its policy in this regard on Taiwan? Why not?

One, in fact, is puzzled why the PRC does not make any claim to represent Chinese elsewhere other than Taiwan (and, of course, Hong Kong and Macao, which are going to unify with the PRC through agreements already negotiated) in view of current global trends. Many scholars and observers of international politics, especially those that perceive the evolution of a "new world order," suggest that blocs may be forming throughout the world based on history and culture. The most widely cited author is Samuel P. Huntington, whose article "The Clash of Civilizations" has become a watershed piece. Some of Huntington's ideas are worth quoting:

---

112. In its relations with most countries the PRC either allows dual citizenship or regards the local Chinese as citizens of the country where they reside. The PRC moved toward this policy in dealings with the countries of Southeast Asia as early as the mid-1950s.

It is my hypothesis that the fundamental source of conflict in this new world will not be primarily ideological or primarily economic. The great divisions among humankind and the dominating source of conflict will be cultural. Nation states will remain the most powerful actors in world affairs, but the principal conflicts of global politics will occur between nations and groups of different civilizations.[113]

And...

During the Cold War the world was divided into the First, Second and Third Worlds. Those divisions are no longer relevant. It is far more meaningful now to group countries not in terms of their political or economic systems or in terms of their level of economic development but rather in terms of their culture and civilization.[114]

Huntington applies these ideas to China...

Common culture ... is clearly facilitating the rapid expansion of the economic relations between the People's Republic of China and Hong Kong, Taiwan, Singapore and the overseas Chinese communities in other Asian countries. With the Cold War over, cultural commonalities increasingly overcome ideological differences, and mainland China and Taiwan move closer together. If cultural commonality is a prerequisite for economic integration, the principal East Asian economic bloc of the future is likely to be centered on China. This bloc is, in fact, already coming into existence.[115]

Nicholas Kristof, the former representative of the *New York Times* in Beijing, said: "...China is becoming a fourth pole in the international system. This is particularly true when one looks at "Greater China," consisting of the People's Republic, Hong Kong and Taiwan."[116]

---

113. Samuel P. Huntington, "The Clash of Civilizations," *Foreign Affairs*, Summer 1993, p. 22.

114. Ibid, p. 23

115. Ibid, p. 28.

116. Nicholas D. Kristof, "The Rise of China," *Foreign Affairs*, December 1993, p. 61.

Kristof's view is supported by another China watcher, William Overholt, who says:

Contemporary geopolitics is being shaped primarily by two economic trends: the collapse of communist economies in Eastern Europe, the former USSR, and Southeast Asia; and the continued dynamism of the Pacific Asian market economies. Both trends have evolved over decades; the second is not less important for lack of the drama of implosion. The current takeoff of one quarter of the human race (China plus the littoral countries) is trans-forming the political structure of the entire globe.[117]

A comment by futurologist John Naisbitt may be equally *a propos*: "It is not hard to imagine that sometime in the next century China could become a confederation of dozens of regions or countries held together by economic interest."[118]

If these forecasts are meaningful, and certainly they may be inasmuch as the global system appears to be in flux or transition, then why are PRC leaders seemingly not paying any attention? Beijing, it would seem, can in many ways represent Chinese all over the world. This is especially true in Asia. One might suggest this: if Chinese leaders in the PRC intends to be a great power and wishes to represent all or most Chinese in the world, and there is some evidence they are thinking in these terms, they should desist from their preoccupion with Taiwan's diplomatic status and should not bully Taiwan. Rather they should start thinking in Greater China or bloc terms. The "Taiwan issue" can and should be solved in a bloc or regional context.

Another issue is worth mentioning at this juncture. Deng Xiaoping is called a nationalist or a national communist and a pragmatist as opposed to an ideologue. He has been under attack by leftist hard-liners since his rise to power in 1978. As a "nationalist" trying to restore China's power and greatness (which declined under Mao due to

117. William H. Overholt, *The Rise of China* (New York: W.W. Norton and Company, 1993), p. 313.

118. John Naisbitt, *Global Paradox*, (New York: William Morrow and Co. 1994), p. 36

economic stagnation and political isolation), Deng is very popular.[119] Yet Deng has not brought stability to China; instead he has created an ideological vacuum and other problems such as income disparity, corruption, etc. And he has enemies who resist change and are quick to exploit mass insecurity caused by Deng-initiated reform.[120] Since most Chinese regard Taiwan, vaguely at least, as a part of China and have not thought this about Singapore, or most can be convinced by the left that Taiwan is being sacrificed by Deng for better relations with the United States, Deng has had to tread cautiously on the Taiwan matter. This in fact seems to offer an explanation for many of the arguments in the "White Paper."

From arguing that the PRC is the sole government of the Chinese people, the authors proceed to assert that there is a formal understanding with nations that maintain diplomatic relations with the PRC "not to establish any ties of an official nature with Taiwan." As noted earlier, most nations that established formal diplomatic relations with the People's Republic of China agreed with, acknowledged, or took note of the PRC's claim to Taiwan. Most did not foreswear any contacts with Taiwan that might be construed as official. In any event, it is nearly impossible to say what official is. What about visits to Taipei by former U.S. President Gerald Ford or former French President Valery Giscard-d 'Estaing? Or Germany's Vice Chancellor Jurgen Mollemann--who was not a former official? Would the visit of a high level official to Taipei such as that of U.S. Trade Representative Carla Hills in 1992 be considered unofficial? Or Vice President Laurel of the Philippines in 1987? Or Prime Minister Datuk

---

119.   It is worth noting that when Deng assumed the role of China's paramount leader in 1978, the PRC's exports were barely one-half of one percent of the world's total—less than in 1920 or in 1950. Now the PRC ranks among the top ten nations of the world. China was also perceived as a poor country under Mao; this is no longer true. For details, see Nicolas R. Lardy, *Foreign Trade and Economic Reform in China, 1978-90 (Washington, DC: Institute for International Economics, 1994)*

120.   Most scholars of PRC politics recognize the presence of factions in the PRC leadership. While they have identified many different factions, most have seen Deng's foreign policies as being opposed by one faction or another and many have observed that he is vulnerable to criticism from whatever faction on the Taiwan issue.

Seri Mahathir Mohamed of Malaysia in 1988? Or Thailand's Vice Premier Amnoen Laleeven in 1993? Or U.S. Secretary of Transportation Federico Pena in late 1994? Or what about visits by Premier Lien Chan and President Lee Teng-hui to several foreign countries in recent months?

Clearly more countries are upgrading their relations with Taipei if these visits mean anything. And contacts between ROC and officials of other nations at other levels are proliferating. Can the PRC stop this? It doesn't seem likely. Can Beijing pretend that these contacts are not at all official? If so, it will have to vigorously exercise its imagination or do a lot of pretending.

The end of the Cold War has brought a new world system which is more universal and less rigid about avoiding contacts with either former enemy or non-bloc nations or actors. Consequently, most countries of the world do not want to adhere to what may be seen as an antiquated if not a petty policy of eschewing contact with Taiwan. Thus, the government of the People's Republic of China is having difficulty enforcing a policy of coercing other nations to avoid any contact with Taipei that might be seen as official. It will clearly face increasing difficulties in the future in this realm.[121]

The authors go on to assert that Taiwan has no right to represent China in the international community. Nor can it establish diplomatic ties or enter into relations of an official nature with foreign countries. To those readers that are knowledgeable of Taiwan and world affairs, this may elicit two reactions.

One, those advocating the independence of Taiwan say the same thing: Taiwan does not have the right to represent China in the international community. The Democratic Progressive Party in Taiwan frequently criticizes Nationalist Party or Kuomintang leaders for this. They say that Taiwan should represent only Taiwan. They contend this is the only way Taiwan can get back into the U.N. and other governmental international organizations. Hence, this document, in still another way, gives support to the advocates of Taiwan independence or separation.

---

121. In fact, the recent changes in U.S. policy allowing visits by high ranking ROC officials may influence other nations to also upgrade relations with Taipei in this and in other respects.

Two, there has been a proliferation of nations in the world, most of them formed from what used to be larger nations or empires, and there are likely to be more. It is a fact that as many more nations have joined the global community in recent years (from 159 in 1984 to 184 by mid-1993) and many more are expected to appear in the global arena--maybe even a thousand. Most nations will grant recognition of some sort easily and without so much regard for past inhibitions or barriers.[122] This being the case, it appears that the authors of this document are going against a powerful, perhaps irresistible, trend in the world, one which will facilitate the ROC's efforts to enter into relations with other nations and political entities throughout the world. One author observes that because Taiwan is ranked the number one nation in the world in terms of economic risk, fifth in financial risk (behind Switzerland, Germany, the U.K. and Japan) and among the top four or five countries in the world that are "most involved" in the global economy, its "persona" looms larger and larger despite China's efforts to isolate the "island republic."[123]

Related (though not logically) to this line of argument, the authors condemn the ROC's "pragmatic diplomacy" as an "attempt to push 'dual recognition' and achieve the objective of creating a situation of 'two Chinas' or 'one China, one Taiwan.'" Actually the term pragmatic diplomacy was used more than a decade ago by Taipei in response to the United States establishing formal diplomatic ties with the People's Republic of China while terminating formal diplomatic recognition of the ROC.[124] Inasmuch as it was done in response to the shock caused by the loss of such relations with the ROC's most

---

122. See Naisbitt, *Global Paradox*, p. 40. Naisbitt predicts the appearance of a thousand nations in the future for a number of reasons, including the spread of democracy throughout the world.

123. Thomas J. Bellows, "The Republic of China's International Relations," *American Journal of Chinese Studies*, October 1992, p. 419.

124. Taipei used the term "substantive diplomacy" frequently after U.S. de-recognition. The term pragmatic was also used at that time and became popular thereafter. For details, see Chi Su, "The International Relations of the Republic of China during the 1990s," in Gerrit Gong and Bih-jaw Lin (eds.), *Sino-American Relations at a time of Change* (Washington, DC: Center for International and Strategic Studies, 1994), pp. 137-39.

important friend and ally (canceled also was the U.S.-Republic of China defense treaty with one year's notice) and happened because of Beijing 's hard-line position against any compromise (such as allowing a U.S. liaison office in Taipei) it may be seen to be a product of actions by the People's Republic of China.

What is more, the United States had informal diplomatic ties with the People's Republic of China before this, in the form of "liaison offices" in Beijing and Washington for six years. Thus, an informal policy of dual recognition was in a sense established by Beijing's initiatives.[125] At minimum it set a precedent.

Further, regarding the issue of dual recognition, academics in Taiwan and the United States began talking about this a long time ago.[126] Clearly the use of the term predates pragmatic diplomacy. It subsequently became more popular as a consequence of Beijing trying to isolate the ROC and its threatening policies toward Taiwan.[127] It later became a policy of the ROC government, yet it was disassociated from a two-China policy or independence.

The authors then accuse the "Taiwan authorities" of lobbying for a formula of "one country, two seats" in international organizations "whose membership is confined to sovereign states." First, it is not true that international organizations limit their membership to sovereign states. Witness Hong Kong's membership in GATT and several other organizations. Also the ROC's membership (assuming for the moment that the ROC does not have sovereignty as the authors argue) in the Asian Development Bank and some other international organizations, as well as Taiwan's participation in the Olympics refutes what the authors say.

---

125. It is difficult to deny that there was a considerable amount of diplomatic formality in this as senior diplomats were appointed by both sides--David Bruce and Huang Zhou--and diplomatic privileges and immunities were conferred on officers and personnel.

126. See Bih-jaw Lin, "Taipei's Search for a New Foreign Policy Approach," in Stephen W. Mosher, ed., *The United States and the Republic of China: Democratic Friends, Strategic Allies, and Economic Partners* (New Brunswick: Transaction Publishers, 1992), pp 32-33.

127. Ibid.

A number of international organizations also allow membership by two governments. Even the United Nations did this in the case of the two Germanys before they unified. One might say the United Nations did this from the onset in the case of the Soviet Union (with extra representation and votes in the General Assembly for the Ukraine and Byelorussia) and does it now in the case of China, since both the People's Republic of China and Singapore are members. Clearly it does it in the case of the two Koreas. This has also happened in the case of a number of other international bodies.

In addition, non-state actors or "would be nation-states" participate in the United Nations and other international organizations. For instance, the Palestine Liberation Organization has observer status in the United Nations. The Southwest African People's Organization had this same status for several years until its representatives became the official representatives of Namibia. It is likely that there will be other such cases in the future.

Mentioned in the document is the fact that Taiwan is a member of the Asian Development Bank (ADB) and the Asia-Pacific Economic Cooperation (APEC) group. But, according to the authors of the document, this is "only an *ad hoc* arrangement" and "cannot constitute a 'model.'" Yet it was made possible by Beijing's cooperation. And it seems much more than *ad hoc*. Moreover, it seems likely that it will happen again, perhaps many times, in the future. Will the process whereby the People's Republic of China and the Republic of China both obtain membership in GATT constitute an *ad hoc* arrangement? What about other global organizations that both join in the future?

Given that in the new world order most international organizations want to and should be universal, and excluding an important nation is counter to that goal, it is not likely that the international community will continue to cooperate with Beijing to isolate the ROC. Taipei has recently been vocal in making the point that its twenty-one million citizens should not be deprived of their human rights by being excluded from representation in the world community. While one can argue that they have perhaps overstated their argument, they certainly have a point. And it is likely that they will win for the ROC some sympathy and even actions by nations as well as international organizations and individual citizens.[128]   The PRC thus seems to be going against the tide of current trends in international politics in this regard.

The authors continue their line of argument by saying that nations having diplomatic ties with the People's Republic of China cannot allow any state-run airlines to land in Taiwan or sell weapons to Taiwan. This again seems to be a petty and mean-spirited effort to isolate and de-legitimize the ROC, and plays into the hands of independence forces there. It also seems not only petty, but impractical to enforce. The distinction between state-run and private airlines is not clear and arms sales are conducted widely by private companies and are often not controlled by the nation-state where they are produced (as Beijing well knows and frequently points when facing accusations about its arms sales). This also seems to be a trend. What is more, many nation-states sell or otherwise transfer arms to third countries after which they are sold or given to other nations. Again the PRC is a good example; it has sold large quantities of weapons to Middle Eastern countries through North Korea and several other countries.

VII

In summation and conclusion, it is difficult to believe that this "White Paper" was written by Chinese scholars over a two-year period.   Rather it appears to have been penned by government bureaucrats and/or Chinese Communist Party officials in a short period of time, or at least without carefully considering the issues or the implication of the arguments made.   Alternatively, scholars wrote the document but it had to fit, or was altered to fit, the official line.

The document reflects the official policy line in Beijing: statism, a multipolar world and xenophobia stemming from fear of what the PRC calls "peaceful evolution" or Western efforts to subvert China's political system.[129] It also mirrors Western criticism of human rights

---

128. See Ross H. Monroe, "Giving Taipei a Place at the Table," *Foreign Affairs*, November/December 1994 for further details.

129. Regarding the PRC's statist foreign policy, see George T. Yu and David J. Longenecker, "The Beijing-Taipei Struggle for International Recognition," *Asian Survey*, May 1994, p. 481 and Samuel S. Kim, "Mainland China and a New World Order," in Bih-jaw Lin and James T. Myers (eds.), *Forces for Change in Contemporary China* (Taipei: Institute of International Relations, 1992), pp. 15-18.

in China. In fact, the "White Paper" contains similar naivete found in another "White Paper" on human rights published two years earlier. In November 1991, the State Council published a booklet that became known as China's "White Paper on Human Rights." It was also published in *Beijing Review* and was given considerable publicity and fanfare. This document said, among other things, that the PRC did not have *any* (italics added) political prisoners.[130] It was widely ridiculed by the international media and scholars and was judged to be a knee-jerk response to an external problem--namely criticism of the PRC's human rights record in the wake of the Tiananmen Massacre.

The "White Paper" under discussion here also makes some unusual, if not contradictory, assumptions, and seems to ignore or not be cognizant of what both PRC leaders and scholars have said elsewhere. It does not recognize that the world may be unipolar in the military sense. It assumes a multipolar view. Yet, Chinese leaders elsewhere have recognized the importance of the U.S. victory in the gulf war and the possibility of a changed nature of warfare in the future--and a unipolar system or a system with unipolar characteristics resulting from it. Various publications have indicated this, not to mention new directions taken in Chinese strategic planning in response.[131]

The document indicates that PRC leaders view the world as nation-state centered, when, in fact, there has been considerable debate among Chinese scholars concerning global trends, including regionalism and a tripolar system based on economic blocs.[132] The authors chose to defend state sovereignty as if it were not being weakened by regionalism and globalism, which are both economic and political

---

130. *Beijing Review*, November 4-10, 1991, pp. 8-45.

131. For some of these views, see the various chapters in Harish Kapur (ed.), *As China Sees the World* (New York: St. Martin's Press, 1987). Also see Cheng Feng and Chen Xiaogong, "The World is in the Transition Period of a New Strategic Pattern Replacing the Old," *Jiefang Junbao* (Liberation Army Daily), June 4, 1991 in *FBIS-China*, June 31, 1991, pp. 11-15.

132. See Samuel S. Kim, "China and the World in Theory and Practice," in Samuel S. Kim (ed.), *Chinese Foreign Policy in the Post-Cold War Era* (Boulder: Westview Press, 1994) and Thomas Robinson and David Shambaugh (eds.), *Chinese Foreign Policy: Theory and Practice* (New York: Oxford University Press, 1993), chapter 1.

trends of considerable potency in the post-Cold War era. They quixotically appear to believe that they can exhort support from the Third World for their Taiwan policy, even though the PRC is hardly in a position to lead Third World countries, and indeed does not seem to be trying. All of this is further evidence scholars had little input in the writing of this document and that it was written to satisfy hard-liners in the CCP.

The "White Paper," in giving such weight to the historical arguments that Taiwan is part of China--since these arguments are not persuasive or can be contradicted or refuted easily--plays into the hands of those advocating Taiwan independence. Historians advocating a separate Taiwan can easily rebut their views; in fact, they have, and are.[133] Even casual readers will see the positions the authors of the "White Paper" have taken are unbalanced and won't stand up to criticism well. Meanwhile historical records are being taken less and less seriously as support for territorial claims in most of the world. And, last but not least, making historical claims that the international community does not consider valid has had some very bad consequences--witness Argentina's claim to the Falkland Islands and Iraq's claim to Kuwait.

The real basis for an argument that Taiwan is part of China is to be found in two World War II declarations, the fact that Japan transferred jurisdiction over Taiwan to the Republic of China according to these declarations in 1945, and that the ROC has governed Taiwan successfully for nearly half a century. These facts, however, favor the position that the ROC is a legitimate regime possessing sovereignty over territory under its control. For political reasons understandable only in terms of domestic politics in the PRC and PRC leaders' fears that Taiwan is winning international recognition and/or that independence forces are gaining strength, the authors ignore this argument. In fact, they seek to refute it. Chinese leaders in Beijing, meanwhile, seem unable to think in terms of Greater China or regional economic blocs that are becoming an essential part of the global system even though these are the keys to a unified China.

The authors of this document have throughout argued that the Republic of China cannot be regarded as a legitimate state with

---

133. See, for example, Hsin-yi Hsiao, "Refuting the Chinese White Paper on "the Taiwan Question and the Reunification of China,'" *Forum*, September 1994.

sovereignty. They are making the same argument in many instances that independence forces make in Taiwan and elsewhere. By so doing they are clearly abetting the forces of independence. The government of the People's Republic of China and high officials of the Chinese Communist Party have long condemned the independence movement in Taiwan in strong and unequivocal terms. For a number of years, moreover, Beijing has proposed negotiations with the Nationalist Party in recognition of their common position against independence. Thus it seems odd now that they have adopted policies that support *d e facto* independence and which in many ways are the same or similar to policies adopted by those who want Taiwan to be separate and independent. Why would they do this? Do they not realize what they are saying?

Their arguments seem, in particular, to be inspired by desperation or fear--that the ROC, by whatever name, is gaining support from the international community and that it may succeed in gaining admission to various international organizations in the future. Indeed Taipei is gaining global support and legitimacy. And it will no doubt have more success in gaining admission to international political or governmental bodies in years to come. It will probably soon be a member of GATT or the World Trade Organization--GATT's new name. Perhaps the Organization for Economic Cooperation and Development and some other global economic agencies will soon follow.

Taipei's diplomatic successes, as noted earlier, stem in considerable part from changes in the global system. The Cold War gave us a bipolar system--a system based on ideological conflict wherein influence derived primarily from military power. That system was made up of two exclusive camps or blocs led by two superpowers. Other nations were relegated to roles of lesser importance. This system is no more. The new system that is evolving is in many respects a universal one--all nations and even non-nation players can and should participate. No one should be excluded. No one should be isolated. Likewise a global economy has been evolving for more than a decade. Trade has, and will continue to link all parts of the world. Power and influence in the new system will come from economic or financial power, not to mention technology and information, more than military strength. Regionalism will be a central part of the new world order, most likely in the form of economic blocs.

Given the fact that the Republic of China ranks number one or number two in the world in foreign exchange position, how can it be excluded from participation in world affairs? Moreover, it is among the top twenty nations in the world in gross national product, the top fifteen in foreign trade and among the top ten in foreign investment. (In Asia, the world's most dynamic area, it is the second largest investor.) And it is the seventh largest provider of economic aid. It would seem reasonable to calculate that, for the good of the international system, such a nation should not be excluded or isolated. In fact, this hardly seems possible.

In addition, it seems the ROC is destined to participate in the same Pacific Rim economic bloc as the PRC. Greater China should be the leader of this bloc? Or will Japan lead? This to a great extent depends on Beijing successfully dealing with the ROC, or not. Why isn't this influencing the thinking of Chinese leaders in Beijing? It is difficult to say. It certainly should be the case.

The authors also appear to be responding to secessionist and splitist movements in various parts of the world, including the former Soviet Union, Yugoslavia and Czechoslovakia. Clearly the world is dividing into more units or more nation-states. It even seems possible this will happen to China. China has been split or fragmented throughout much of its history. There are danger signals now. In fact, PRC leaders may fear independence forces in Taiwan will encourage such tendencies in the PRC.[134] Perhaps they feel they must take a tough line toward Taiwan lest its presence in the world community encourage secessionist movements in the PRC. In this context, one must wonder if Beijing would be better advised to try to counter these centrifugal forces by building more and better economic ties and friendly relations of all kinds, rather

---

134. See Gerald Segal, "China's Changing Shape," *Foreign Affairs*, May/June 1994, pp. 43-58, especially p. 49. Segal cites such evidence as a recent "rice war" in China during which provincial leaders in Guangdong used military units to ensure access to cheap rice from Hunan, various provinces setting up inspection stations on rail lines to stop or tax goods from other provinces, and the government of Guangdong buying oil on the international spot market rather than going through Beijing. He also mentions increasing talk in China about internal chaos, regional protectionism and military leaders mentioning the possibility of civil war.

than resisting what appear to be inevitable forces of history and/or international politics.

It may be that uncertainty in the PRC's internal politics due to a pending succession may help explain its odd position and its inconsistent policy toward Taiwan. Why would it issue a "White Paper" that is essentially hostile and threatening toward the ROC when its diplomats have recently held talks with ROC leaders (in Singapore) that have resolved some problems between them and offer hope of much more. Perhaps because it is not wise to be too friendly toward Taipei when a hard-line policy may be in the wind. Typically leaders contending for power don't want to be accused of being too soft.[135]

Another aspect of the new world order is that democracy is the favored political system. It is the "wave of the future." Totalitarian communism has been relegated to the historical trash bin. In fact, communism is now seen as an antiquated, not to mention barbaric, system. In the course of building democracy, many nations need a model. China, perhaps more than other countries, needs a model. Taiwan, because of its rapid political modernization and its smooth transition to democracy, is a prototype for political development of the democratic mold for developing countries. This is especially true of those that find it difficult to copy the experience of Western nations that have different histories and political cultures and took two hundred years to build democracies. Hence they look to nations like the ROC. This being the case, does it make sense to shun Taiwan or try to keep other nations from interacting with it? Certainly Beijing has used and has benefitted from using the Taiwan model. Why shouldn't it do this even more in the future?

Then, one must consider what would happen if the PRC does what it says it will do (under certain circumstances): use military force to resolve the "Taiwan question." While the leaders of the People's Republic of China vow they will not use nuclear weapons against Taiwan, that promise might be rescinded in the course of a conflict that becomes too costly. This, in fact, cannot be discounted as a possibility

---

135. An expected succession crisis may also explain the hard stance taken by General Secretary Jiang Zemin at the APEC meeting in November 1993 and Beijing's attitude toward Hong Kong, especially Chris Patten, and on nuclear testing and arms sales.

even though PRC leaders say they will never use nuclear weapons on their own people.[136] The use of nuclear weapons would cause a serious regression in world politics--back to a world dominated by military force. Furthermore, the PRC would become the first nation to use nuclear weapons in the post-WWII period and the first ever to use weapons of mass destruction against its own people. In so doing it would become a pariah nation of the most infamous kind. The result would certainly be many nations of the world eschewing contacts with the People's Republic of China prompting its isolation in the world community. This happened to some degree as a result of the Tiananmen Massacre. Using nuclear weapons against Taiwan would have the same effect--multiplied by many, many fold. Clearly this would not be a propitious event.

The same thing would probably occur to a somewhat lesser extent, but still to a considerable degree, were Beijing to use conventional forces against Taiwan. If the United States were to enter the conflict, which it is obligated to do by law, a serious conflict would ensue between two nuclear powers.[137] Even if nuclear weapons were not used, two major world powers, i.e. the U.S. and the PRC, would probably be seriously alienated for many years. This would not be conducive to a stable world system. If the U.S. did not fulfill its obligation to help Taiwan, Taiwan would be invaded--but not before perhaps a million or more people perished. A million or two, perhaps more, people would also become refugees. The rest would most likely be forced to live under military rule for some years.

This probably explains in large part why in 1992 both the U.S. and France decided to sell sophisticated fighter planes to Taipei. In

---

136. The statements by PRC leaders that they will not use nuclear weapons against Taiwan might also be interpreted to mean that they really do not want Taiwan. Some in the Chinese leadership are not in a hurry and thus would sincerely take this position. For others it is probably not true. Certainly there is an inconsistency in saying that foreign countries (meaning the United States) have kept Taiwan from being unified and saying that the U.S. would not come to the PRC's rescue in the event of a Soviet nuclear attack. PRC officials have said both.

137. It is worth repeating in this context, that recently President Clinton signed an authorization bill that had a provision attached stating the Taiwan Relations Act, which contains provisions about guaranteeing Taiwan's security, takes precedence over the communiques concluded with the PRC.

contrast to past sales that were limited, canceled, or not renewed due to PRC pressure, these sales went forward. And they have been followed by other arms sales. Clearly Beijing seems to have lost its influence over two important nations on this important issue. Both Washington and Paris perceive that preserving a balance of power in the Taiwan Strait will help prevent conflict there. Most other nations seem to agree.

That the use of force to resolve the issue of sovereignty between Beijing and Taipei is very ominous is clearly realized by almost everyone in Taiwan. The government of the ROC in recognition of this fact has renounced the use of force to unite China. The concept of one China, two governments or two political entities, which is the ROC formula for dealing with the reality of two Chinese states and the need for dealing with this problem in a peaceful manner, arises from this. It may also result in accelerated efforts to create a one China, one Taiwan situation or push Taiwan in the direction of independence. Some in Taiwan say this.

Similarly, one should not be oblivious to the ROC's desire to preserve its sovereignty--just as any other nation would do. Leaders in Beijing need to realize that the population of Taiwan, not to mention its political leaders, are committed to maintaining their sovereign rights. They are not unlike Chinese in Beijing in this respect, even though Taiwan is much more international in outlook. Sovereignty to Taiwan can mean either separation or peacefully linking up with the PRC. If Taipei opts for the latter it will have to be convinced to do so only over time and probably because of the success of Greater China and global trends. Historical or emotional arguments to the effect that China is one nation and must be unified are not enough to bring about a change of mind about sovereignty. Neither will threats or intimidation work; they are counterproductive. If one assesses the present attitudes of the population of Taiwan about unification with the PRC, it is this: keep the *status quo*. This means that they cannot decide and that it is not the right time to try to solve this problem.

Another global trend that needs to be discussed in this context is the decentralization of political authority. This makes democracy possible. It also reflects the role of political institutions in making nations or political units competitive in the global economy. The

People's Republic of China has certainly found this to be true.[138] In fact, realizing this trend has been an essential ingredient of Beijing's successful economic growth. Would China have grown like it has economically in recent years if central planning and totalitarian political control by the core of the Chinese Communist Party were still in place? Of course not. Thus, one might say that the Republic of China represents simply a greater degree of decentralization of political authority in China. Among China's provinces the most autonomous or independent ones, and the most integrated to the world economy, are the most successful ones in terms of economic growth (and incidently human rights). This should be instructive.

If China is to be unified, and that has occurred many times in history, it will happen in the twenty first century because of economic forces. Greater China is, or can be, as has already been noted, one of the major players in international politics. It is easy to imagine (simply by making projections from current trends) that Greater China will surpass the United States and the European Community in the production of goods and services in a few years.[139] In a short span of time it will be the biggest trading entity in the world and will be its biggest consumer, and it will have the planet's biggest military force, etc. Is it possible that Taiwan will not want to be a part of this? Is it possible that the views of independence advocates in Taiwan will prevail such that Taiwan shuns participation in what may be the world's most important event in the twenty-first century?

Trade and investment have broken down barriers that have been erected by the Cold War. This will continue to happen. Additional agreements between the two sides on trade and investments will certainly facilitate more economic links. But this can best be done if the People's Republic of China recognizes the ROC, by whatever name, as a legally constituted government and allows it to participate in world affairs as a legitimate sovereign nation-state. The alternative is to create a myth that Taiwan and its population of twenty-one million

---

138. See Victor C. Falkenheim, "Chinese Politics in Transition," in Victor C. Falkenheim (ed.), *Chinese Politics from Mao to Deng* (New York: Paragon House, 1989), pp. 6 & 7.

139. This view has been expressed in a number of magazine and journal articles on China. A December 1992 issue of the *Economist* was one of the first. The "War of the Worlds" piece in the October 1, 1994 *Economist* is another.

(larger than three-fourths of the nations that are members of the United Nations) do not exist or do not have any of the rights associated with nationhood, while adopting a policy of isolating an important economic and political player when the new global order does not welcome that.

The only reasonable policy for the People's Republic of China to accomplish reunification is one of promoting economic ties, building better political relations in the context of bloc affairs and allowing Taipei a greater amount of latitude and freedom to play a more formal and more legitimate role in world affairs, expecting that it will freely and voluntarily become a part of Greater China when the conditions are right.

The Taiwan Question and the Reunification of China

Taiwan Affairs Office & Information Office
State Council
The People's Republic of China

August 1993, Beijing, China

Foreword

It is the sacred right of each and every sovereign State and a fundamental principle of international law to safeguard national unity and territorial integrity. The Charter of the United Nations specifically stipulates that the United Nations and its Members shall refrain from any action against the territorial integrity or political independence of any of its Members or any State and shall not intervene in matters which are essentially within the domestic jurisdiction of any State. The United Nations Declaration on Principles of International Law Concerning Friendly Relations and Cooperation Among States in Accordance with the Charter of the United Nations points out that any attempt aimed at the partial or total disruption of the national unity, territorial integrity or political independence of a State or country is incompatible with the purposes and principles of the Charter of the United Nations.

The modern history of China was a record of subjection to aggression, dismemberment and humiliation by foreign powers. It was also a chronicle of the Chinese people's valiant struggles for national independence and in defense of their state sovereignty, territorial integrity and national dignity. The origin and evolution of the Taiwan question are closely linked with that period of history. For various reasons Taiwan is still separated from the mainland. Unless and until this state of affairs is brought to an end, the trauma on the Chinese nation will not be healed and the Chinese people's struggle for national reunification and territorial integrity will continue.

What is the present state of the Taiwan question? What is the crux of the problem? What are the position and views of the Chinese Government regarding the settlement of this issue? In order to facilitate

73

a better understanding by the international community, it is necessary to elucidate the following points.

I. Taiwan—An Inalienable Part of China

Lying off the southeastern coast of the China mainland, Taiwan is China's largest island and forms an integral whole with the mainland.

Taiwan has belonged to China since ancient times. It was known as Yizhou or Liuqiu in antiquities. Many historical records and annals documented the development of Taiwan by the Chinese people in earlier periods. References to this effect were to be found, among others, in *Seaboard Geographic Gazetteer* compiled more than 1,700 years ago by Shen Ying of the State of Wu during the period of the Three Kingdoms. This was the world's earliest written account of Taiwan. Several expeditions, each numbering over ten thousand men, had been sent to Taiwan by the State of Wu (third century A.D.) and the Sui Dynasty (seventh century A.D.) respectively. Since the early seventeenth century the Chinese people began to step up the development of Taiwan. Their numbers topped one hundred thousand at the end of the century. By 1893 (19th year of the reign of Qing Emperor Guangxu) their population exceeded 2.54 million people in 507,000 or more households. That was a 25-fold increase in 200 years. They brought in a more advanced mode of production and settled the whole length and breadth of Taiwan. Thanks to the determined efforts and hard toil of the pioneers, the development of the island as a whole greatly accelerated. This was the historical fact of how Taiwan, like the other parts of China, came to be opened up and settled by the Chinese people of various nationalities. From the very beginning the Taiwan society derived from the source of the Chinese cultural tradition. This basic fact had not changed even during the half century of Japanese occupation. The history of Taiwan's development is imbued with the blood, sweat, and ingenuity of the Chinese people including the local ethnic minorities.

Chinese governments of different periods set up administrative bodies to exercise jurisdiction over Taiwan. As early as in the mid-12th century the Song Dynasty set up a garrison in Penghu, putting the territory under the jurisdiction of Jinjiang County of Fukien's Quanzhou Prefecture. The Yuan Dynasty installed an agency of patrol and inspection in Penghu to administer the territory. During the mid- and late 16th century the Ming Dynasty reinstated the once abolished agency and sent reinforcements to Penghu in order to ward off foreign invaders. In 1662 (first year of the reign of Qing Emperor Kangxi) General Zheng Chenggong (known in the West as Koxinga) instituted Chengtian Prefecture on Taiwan. Subsequently, the Qing government expanded the administrative structure in Taiwan, thereby strengthening its rule over the territory. In 1684 (23rd year of the reign of Emperor Kangxi) a Taiwan-Xiamen Patrol Command and a Taiwan Prefecture Administration were set up under the jurisdiction of Fukian Province. These in turn exercised jurisdiction over three counties on the island: Taiwan (present-day Tainan), Fengshan (present-day Gaoxiong) and Zhuluo (present day Jiayi). In 1714 (53rd year of the reign of Emperor Kangxi) the Qing government ordered the mapping of Taiwan to determine its size. In 1721 (60th year of the reign of Emperor Kangxi) an office of imperial supervisor for inspecting Taiwan was created and the Taiwan Xiamen Patrol Command was renamed Prefecture Administration of Taiwan and Xiamen, incorporating the subsequently-created Zhanghua County and Danshui Canton. In 1727 (5th year of the reign of Emperor Yongzheng) the administration on the island was reconstituted as the Prefecture Administration of Taiwan (which was later renamed Prefecture Command for Patrol of Taiwan) and incorporated the new Penghu Canton. The territory then became officially known as Taiwan. In order to upgrade the administration of Taiwan, the Qing government created Taipei Prefecture, Jilong Canton and three counties of Danshui, Xinzhu and Yilan in 1875 (Ist year of the reign of Emperor Guangxu). In 1885 (llth year of the reign of Emperor Guangxu), the government formally made Taiwan a full province covering three prefectures and one subprefecture and incorporating 11 counties and 5 cantons. Liu Mingchuan was appointed first Governor of Taiwan. During his tenure of office, railways were laid, mines opened, telegraph service installed, merchant ships built, industries started and new-style schools set up. Considerable social, economic and cultural advancement in Taiwan was achieved as a result.

After the Chinese people's victory in the war against Japanese aggression in 1945, the Chinese government reinstated its administrative authority in Taiwan Province.

Chinese on both sides of the Taiwan Straits carried out a prolonged, unremitting struggle against foreign invasion and occupation of Taiwan. Since the late 15th century Western colonialists started to grab and conquer colonies in a big way. In 1624 (4th year of the reign of Ming Emperor Tianqi) Dutch colonialists invaded and occupied the southern part of Taiwan. Two years later Spanish colonialists seized the northern part of Taiwan. In 1642 (15th year of the reign of Ming Emperor Chongzhen) the Dutch evicted the Spaniards and took over north Taiwan. The Chinese people on both sides of the Straits waged various forms of struggle including armed insurrections against the invasion and occupation of Taiwan by foreign colonialists. In 1661 (18th year of the reign of Qing Emperor Shunzhi) General Zheng Chenggong (Koxinga) led an expedition to Taiwan and expelled the Dutch colonialists from the island in the following year.

Japan launched a war of aggression against China in 1894 (20th year of the reign of Qing Emperor Guangxu). In the ensuing year, as a result of defeat the Qing government was forced to sign the Treaty of Shimonoseki, ceding Taiwan to Japan. This wanton betrayal and humiliation shocked the whole nation and touched off a storm of protests. A thousand or more candidates from all 18 provinces including Taiwan who had assembled in Beijing for the Imperial Examination signed a strongly worded petition opposing the ceding of Taiwan. In Taiwan itself, people wailed and bemoaned the betrayal and went on general strikes. General Liu Yongfu and others of the garrison command stood with Taiwan compatriots and put up a fierce fight against the Japanese landing forces. To support this struggle, people on the mainland, particularly in the southeastern region, showed their solidarity by generous donations or organizing volunteers to Taiwan to fight the Japanese forces. Taiwan compatriots never ceased their dauntless struggle throughout the Japanese occupation. Initially, they formed insurgent groups to wage guerrilla warfare for as long as seven years. When the Revolution of 1911 overthrew the Qing monarchy they in turn lent support to their mainland compatriots by staging more than a dozen armed insurrections. The 1920s and 1930s witnessed surging waves of mass action sweeping across the island against Japanese colonial rule.

In 1937 the Chinese people threw themselves into an all-out war of resistance against Japanese aggression. In its declaration of war against Japan, the Chinese Government proclaimed that all treaties, conventions, agreements, and contracts regarding relations between China and Japan, including the Treaty of Shimonoseki, had been abrogated. The declaration stressed that China would recover Taiwan,

Penghu and the four northeastern provinces. After eight years of grueling war against Japanese aggression the Chinese people won final victory and recovered the lost territory of Taiwan in 1945. Taiwan compatriots displayed an outburst of passion and celebrated the great triumph of their return to the fold of the motherland by setting off big bangs of fireworks and performing rites to communicate the event to their ancestors.

The international community has acknowledged the fact that Taiwan belongs to China. The Chinese people's war of resistance against Japanese aggression, being part of the world-wide struggle against Fascism, received extensive support from people all over the world. During the Second World War China, the United States, the Soviet Union, Great Britain, France and others formed an alliance to oppose the Axis of Germany, Japan and Italy. The Cairo Declaration issued by China, the United States and Great Britain on 1 December 1943 stated: "It is the purpose of the three great Allies that Japan shall be stripped of all the islands in the Pacific which she has seized or occupied since the beginning of the First World War in 1914, and that all the territories Japan has stolen from the Chinese, such as Manchuria, Formosa (Taiwan) and the Pescadores (Penghu), shall be restored to China." The Potsdam Proclamation signed by China, the United States and Great Britain on 26 July 1945 (subsequently adhered to by the Soviet Union) reiterated: "The terms of the Cairo Declaration shall be carried out." On 15 August of the same year, Japan declared surrender. The instrument of Japan's surrender stipulated that "Japan hereby accepts the provisions in the declaration issued by the heads of the Governments of the United States, China and Great Britain on July 26, 1945 at Potsdam, and subsequently adhered to by the Union of Soviet Socialist Republics." On 25 October the ceremony for accepting Japan's surrender in Taiwan Province of the China war theater of the Allied powers was held in Taipei. On the occasion, the chief officer for accepting the surrender proclaimed on behalf of the Chinese government that from that day forward Taiwan and the Penghu Archipelago had again been incorporated formally into the territory of China and that the territory, people, and administration had now been placed under the sovereignty of China. From that point in time forward, Taiwan and Penghu had been put back under the jurisdiction of Chinese sovereignty.

Since the founding of the People's Republic of China, 157 countries have established diplomatic relations with China. All these countries recognize that there is only one China and the Government of the People's Republic of China is the sole legal government of China and Taiwan is part of China.

II. Origin of the Taiwan Question

Taiwan was returned to China *de jure* and *de facto* at the end of the Second World War. It became an issue only as an aftermath of the ensuing anti-popular civil war started by Kuomintang, and more especially because of intervention by foreign forces.

Taiwan question and civil war launched by Kuomintang. During the war of resistance against Japanese aggression the Chinese Communist Party and other patriotic groups pressed Kuomintang into a national united front with the Communist Party to fight Japanese imperialist aggression. After victory of the war the two Parties should have joined hands to work for the resurgence of China. But the Kuomintang clique headed by Chiang Kai-shek flouted the people's fervent aspirations for peace and for building an independent, democratic and prosperous new China. Relying on U.S. support, this clique tore up the 10 October 1945 agreement between the two Parties and launched an all-out anti-popular civil war. The Chinese people were compelled to respond with a people's liberation war which was to last more than three years under the leadership of the Communist Party. Since the Kuomintang clique had already been spurned by the people of all nationalities for its reign of terror, the government of the "Republic of China" in Nanjing was finally overthrown by the Chinese people. The People's Republic of China was proclaimed on 1 October 1949 and the Government of the new People's Republic became the sole legal government of China. A group of military and political officials of the Kuomintang clique took refuge in Taiwan and, with the support of the then U.S. administration, created the division between the two sides of the Straits.

Taiwan question and responsibility of the United States. Against the backdrop of East-West confrontation in the wake of the Second World War and guided by its conceived global strategy and national interest considerations, the U.S. government gave full support to the Kuomintang, providing it with money, weapons and advisors to carry on the civil war and block the advance of the Chinese people's revolution. However, the U.S. government never achieved its objective. The White Paper on United States Relations with China released by the Department of State in 1949 and Secretary of State Dean Acheson's letter of transmittal to President Harry S. Truman had to admit this. Dean Acheson lamented in his letter: "The unfortunate but inescapable fact is that the ominous result of the civil war in China was beyond the control of the government of the United States... Nothing that was left undone by this country has contributed to it. It was the product of internal Chinese forces, forces which this country tried to influence but could not."

At the time of the founding of the People's Republic of China the then U.S. administration could have pulled itself from the quagmire of China's civil war. But it failed to do so. Instead, it adopted a policy of isolation and containment of New China. When the Korean War broke out, it started armed intervention in the inter-Taiwan Straits relations which were entirely China's internal affairs. On 27 June 1950 President Truman announced: "I have ordered the Seventh Fleet to prevent any attack on Formosa." Thus the Seventh Fleet invaded the Taiwan Straits and the U.S. 13th Air Force set up base in Taiwan. In December 1954 the U.S. concluded with the Taiwan authorities a so-called mutual defense treaty placing China's Taiwan Province under U.S. "protection." The erroneous policy of the U.S. government of continued interference in China's internal affairs led to prolonged and intense confrontation in the Taiwan Straits area and henceforth the Taiwan question became a major dispute between China and the United States.

In order to ease tension in the Taiwan Straits area and seek ways of solving the dispute between the two countries, the Chinese Government started dialogues with the United States from the mid-1950s onwards. The two countries held 136 sessions of talks at ambassadorial level from August 1955 to February 1970. However, no progress had been made in that period on the key issue of easing and removing tension in the Taiwan Straits area. It was not until the late 1960s and early 1970s when the international situation had undergone changes and as New China had gained in strength that the U.S. began to readjust its China policy and the relations between the two countries started a thawing. In October 1971 the United Nations General Assembly adopted at its 26th session Resolution 2758 which restored all the lawful rights of the People's Republic of China in the United Nations and expelled the "representatives" of the Taiwan authorities from the U.N. President Richard Nixon visited China in February 1972 in the course of which the two countries issued a joint communique in Shanghai stating that: "The U.S. side declared; the United States acknowledges that all Chinese on either side of the Taiwan Straits maintain there is but one China and that Taiwan is a part of China. The United States Government does not challenge that position."

In December 1978 the U.S. Government accepted the three principles proposed by the Chinese Government for the establishment of diplomatic relations between the two countries, namely, the United States should sever "diplomatic relations" and abrogate the "mutual defense treaty" with the Taiwan authorities and withdraw U.S. military forces from Taiwan. On 1 January 1979 China and the United States formally established diplomatic relations. The Communique on the Establishment of Diplomatic Relations said that: "The United States of America recognizes the Government of the People's Republic of China as the sole legal government of China. Within this context, the people of the United States will maintain cultural, commercial and other unofficial relations with the people of Taiwan .... The Government of the United States of America acknowledges the Chinese position that there is but one China and Taiwan is part of China." Normalization of Sino-U.S. relations was thus achieved.

Regrettably, however, scarcely three months after the event, a so-called Taiwan Relations Act was passed by the U.S. Congress and signed into law by the President. A domestic legislation of the U.S. as it was, this Act contained many clauses that contravened the communique on the establishment of diplomatic relations between China and the U.S. and the principles of international law, and seriously prejudiced the rights and interests of the Chinese people. Invoking this legislation, the U.S. Government has continued its arms sales to Taiwan, interference in China's internal affairs and obstruction to Taiwan's reunification with the mainland.

In order to resolve the issue of U.S. arms sales to Taiwan, the Chinese and the U.S. governments negotiated and reached an agreement on 17 August 1982. A communique bearing the same date became the third joint communique governing Sino-U.S. relations. In that communique the U.S. Government stated that: "It does not seek to carry out a long-term policy of arms sales to Taiwan, that its arms sales to Taiwan will not exceed, either in qualitative or in quantitative terms, the level of those supplied in recent years since the establishment of diplomatic relations between the United States and China and that it intends gradually to reduce its sale of arms to Taiwan, leading, over a period of time, to a final resolution." Yet in the past dozen or more years, the U.S. Government has not only failed to implement the communique in earnest, but has repeatedly contravened it. In September 1992 the U.S. Government even decided to sell 150 F-16 high-performance fighter aircraft to Taiwan. This action of the U.S. Government has added a new stumbling block in the way of the development of Sino-U.S. relations and settlement of the Taiwan question.

It is clear from the foregoing that the U.S. Government is responsible for holding up the settlement of the Taiwan question. Since the 1970s many Americans of vision and goodwill in or outside the administration have contributed much by way of helping to resolve the differences between China and the U.S. on the Taiwan question. The aforesaid three joint communiques testify to their effort and contribution of which the Chinese Government and people are highly appreciative. On the other hand, one cannot fail to note that there are people in the U.S. who still do not want to see a reunified China. They have cooked up various pretexts and exerted influence to obstruct the settlement of the Taiwan question.

The Chinese Government is convinced that the American and the Chinese peoples are friendly to each other and that the normal development of the relations between the two countries accords with the long-term interests and common aspiration of both peoples. Both countries should cherish the three hard-won joint communiques guiding the development of bilateral relations. As long as both sides abide by the principles enshrined in those communiques, respect each other and set store by their overall common interests, it will not be difficult to settle the Taiwan question that has been left over from history and Sino-U.S. relations will surely see steady improvement and development ahead.

III. The Chinese Government's Basic Position Regarding Settlement of the Taiwan Question

To settle the Taiwan question and achieve national reunification—this is a sacrosanct mission of the entire Chinese people.

The Chinese Government has persistently worked towards this end since the founding of the People's Republic. Its basic position on this question is: peaceful reunification; one country, two systems.

Peaceful reunification; one country, two systems—how has this position been formulated? The Chinese Government conceived a peaceful settlement of the Taiwan question as early as in the 1950s. In May 1955 the late Premier Zhou Enlai said at a NPC Standing Committee meeting that two alternatives were open to the Chinese people for the solution of the Taiwan question—by resort to war or by peaceful means. The Chinese people would strive for a peaceful solution wherever possible, he affirmed. In April 1956 the late Chairman Mao Zedong put forward thoughts for policy-making such as "peace is the best option," "all patriots are of one family" and "it is never too late to join the ranks of patriots." However, those wishes have not come to fruition for reasons such as interference by foreign forces.

Major changes took place in and outside China in the 1970s. Diplomatic ties were established and relations normalized between China and the United States. The Third Plenary Session of the Eleventh Central Committee of the Communist Party of China decided to shift the focus of the work of the Party and the State to the economic modernization program. In the meantime, people on both sides of the Taiwan Straits, compatriots of Hong Kong and Macao as well as overseas Chinese and people of Chinese descent all expressed their fervent hope that the two sides of the Straits would join hands to work for a resurgence of China. It was against this historical background that the Chinese Government formulated the position of "peaceful reunification; one country, two systems". The position takes the overall national interests and the future of the country into consideration. It respects history as well as the prevailing situation. It is realistic and takes care of the interests of all.

On 1 January 1979 the Standing Committee of the National People's Congress of the People's Republic of China issued a message to compatriots in Taiwan, pronouncing the Chinese Government's basic position regarding peaceful settlement of the Taiwan question. It called for the holding of talks between the two sides of the Straits to seek an end to the military confrontation. It pledged that in the pursuit of national reunification, the Government "will respect the *status quo* on

Taiwan and the views of people of all walks of life there and adopt reasonable policies and measures".

In a statement on 30 September 1981 the late Chairman Ye Jianying of the NPC Standing Committee further elaborated the policy and principles for the settlement of the Taiwan question. He affirmed that "after the country is reunified, Taiwan can enjoy a high degree of autonomy as a special administrative region" and proposed that talks be held on an equal footing between the ruling Parties on each side of the Straits, namely, the Chinese Communist Party and the Kuomintang.

Referring to Ye Jianying's remarks, Chinese leader Deng Xiaoping pointed out on 11 January 1982 that this in effect meant "one country, two systems", i.e., on the premise of national reunification, the main body of the nation would continue with its socialist system while Taiwan could maintain capitalism.

On 26 June 1983 Deng Xiaoping further enunciated the concept of peaceful reunification, stressing that the crucial point was national reunification. He went on to expound the Government's policy on reunification and on the creation of a Taiwan special administrative region.

On 12 October 1992 General Secretary Jiang Zemin of the C.P.C. Central Committee pointed out: "We shall work steadfastly for the great cause, adhering to the principles of peaceful reunification and 'one country, two systems' ...We reiterate that the Chinese Communist Party is ready to establish contact with the Chinese Kuomintang at the earliest possible date to create conditions for talks on officially ending the state of hostility between the two sides of the Taiwan Straits and gradually realizing peaceful reunification. Representatives from other parties, organizations and all circles on both sides of the Taiwan Straits could be invited to join in such talks."

Basic contents of "peaceful reunification; one country, two systems." This position is an important component of the theory and practice of building socialism with Chinese characteristics and a fundamental state policy of the Chinese Government which will not change for a long time to come. Its basic contents are as follows:

1. **Only one China.** There is only one China in the world, Taiwan is an inalienable part of China and the seat of China's central government is in Beijing. This is a universally recognized fact as well as the premise for a peaceful settlement of the Taiwan question.

The Chinese Government is firmly against any words or deeds designed to split China's sovereignty and territorial integrity. It opposes "two Chinas", "one China, one Taiwan", "one country, two governments" or any attempt or act that could lead to "independence of Taiwan." The Chinese people on both sides of the Straits all believe that there is only one China and espouse national reunification. Taiwan's status as an inalienable part of China has been determined and cannot be changed. "Self-determination" for Taiwan is out of the question.

2. Coexistence of two systems. On the premise of one China, socialism on the mainland and capitalism on Taiwan can coexist and develop side by side for a long time without one swallowing up the other. This concept has largely taken account of the actual situation in Taiwan and practical interests of our compatriots there. It will be a unique feature and important innovation in the state system of a reunified China.

After reunification, Taiwan's current socio-economic system, its way of life as well as economic and cultural ties with foreign countries can remain unchanged. Private property, including houses and land as well as business ownership, legal inheritance and overseas Chinese and foreign investments on the island will all be protected by law.

3. A high degree of autonomy. After reunification, Taiwan will become a special administrative region. It will be distinguished from the other provinces or regions of China by its high degree of autonomy. It will have its own administrative and legislative powers, an independent judiciary and the right of adjudication on the island. It will run its own party, political, military, economic and financial affairs. It may conclude commercial and cultural agreements with foreign countries and enjoy certain rights in foreign affairs. It may keep its military forces and the mainland will not dispatch troops or administrative personnel to the island. On the other hand, representatives of the government of the special administrative region and those from different circles of Taiwan may be appointed to senior posts in the central government and participate in the running of national affairs.

4. Peace negotiations. It is the common aspiration of the entire Chinese people to achieve reunification of the country by peaceful means through contacts and negotiations. People on both sides of the Straits are all Chinese. It would be a great tragedy for all if China's territorial integrity and sovereignty were to be split and its people were to be drawn into a fratricide. Peaceful reunification will greatly enhance the cohesion of the Chinese nation. It will facilitate Taiwan's socio-economic stability and development and promote the resurgence and prosperity of China as a whole.

In order to put an end to hostility and achieve peaceful reunification, the two sides should enter into contracts and negotiations at the earliest possible date. On the premise of one China, both sides can discuss any subject, including the modality of negotiations, the question of what Parties, groups and personalities may participate as ell as any other matters of concern to the Taiwan side. So long as the two sides sit down and talk, they will always be able to find a mutually acceptable solution

Taking into account the prevailing situation on both sides of the Straits, the Chinese Government has proposed that pending reunification the two sides should, according to the principle of mutual respect, complementary and mutual benefit, actively promote economic cooperation and other exchanges. Direct trade, postal, air and shipping services and two-way visits should be started in order to pave the way for the peaceful reunification of the country.

Peaceful reunification is a set policy of the Chinese Government. However, any sovereign state is entitled to use any means it deems necessary, including military ones, to uphold its sovereignty and territorial integrity. The Chinese Government is under no obligation to undertake any commitment to any foreign power or people intending to split China as to what means it might use to handle its own domestic affairs.

It should be pointed out that the Taiwan question is purely an internal affair of China and bears no analogy to the cases of Germany and Korea which were brought about as a result of international accords at the end of the Second World War. Therefore, the Taiwan question should not be placed on a par with the situation of Germany or Korea. The Chinese Government has always opposed applying the German or Korean formulas to Taiwan. The Taiwan question should and entirely can be resolved judiciously through bilateral consultations and within the framework of one China.

IV. Relations Across Taiwan Straits: Evolution and Stumbling Blocks

The present division between the two sides of the Taiwan Straits is a misfortune for the Chinese nation. All the Chinese people are yearning for an early end to this agonizing situation.

In order to enable normal movement of people across the Straits and to achieve reunification of the country, the Chinese Government has made proposals towards this end and, at the same time, adopted measures to step up the development of inter-Straits relations.

On the political plane, policy adjustments have been made with a view to breaking down the mentality of hostility. The Supreme People's Court and the Supreme People's Procuratorate have decided respectively that people who had gone to Taiwan would no longer be prosecuted for offenses prior to the founding of the People's Republic of China.

On the military plane, initiatives have been taken to ease military confrontation across the Straits. Shelling of Jinmen and other islands have been discontinued. Some forward defense positions and observation posts along the Fujian coast have been transformed into economic development zones or tourist attractions.

On the economic plane, doors have been flung open to facilitate the flow of goods and people. Businessmen from Taiwan are welcome to invest or trade on the mainland. They are accorded preferential treatment and legal safeguards.

The Chinese Government has also adopted a positive attitude and taken measures to encourage bilateral exchanges and cooperation in areas such as two-way travels, post and communications as well as scientific, cultural, sports and academic and journalistic activities. A non-governmental Association for Relations Across the Taiwan Straits has been set up and authorized by the Government to liaise with the Straits Exchange Foundation and other relevant non-governmental bodies in Taiwan for the purpose of upholding the legitimate rights and interests of people on both sides and promoting inter-Straits relations.

Such policies and measures of the Chinese Government have won the understanding and support of more and more Taiwan compatriots, compatriots in Hong Kong and Macao as well as overseas Chinese and people of Chinese descent. On their part, Taiwan compatriots have contributed tremendously to the development of inter-Straits relations. In recent years the Taiwan authorities have in turn made readjustments in their policy regarding the mainland. They have taken steps to ease the situation, such as allowing people to visit relatives on the mainland, gradually reducing the restrictions on people-to-people exchanges and contact, expanding indirect trade, permitting indirect investment and cutting red tape in inter-Straits post, telecommunications and bank remittance services. All these are conducive to better interchanges. The past few years have witnessed rapid growth of economic relations and trade as well as increasing mutual visits and sundry exchanges across the Straits. The Wang Daohan--Koo Chen-fu Talks in April 1993 resulted in four agreements, marking a step forward of historic significance in inter-Straits relations. Thus an atmosphere of relaxation prevails in the Taiwan Straits for the first time in the past four decades. This is auspicious to peaceful reunification.

It should be pointed out that notwithstanding a certain measure of easing up by the Taiwan authorities, their current policy *vis-a-vis* the mainland still seriously impedes the development of relations across the Straits as well as the reunification of the country. They talk about the necessity of a reunified China, but their deeds are always a far cry from the principle of one China. They try to prolong Taiwan's separation from the mainland and refuse to hold talks on peaceful reunification. They have even set up barriers to curb the further development of the interchanges across the Straits.

In recent years the clamors for "Taiwan independence" on the island have become shriller, casting a shadow over the course of relations across the Straits and the prospect of peaceful reunification of the country. The "Taiwan independence" fallacy has a complex social-historical root and international background. But the Taiwan authorities have, in effect, abetted this fallacy by its own policy of rejecting peace negotiations, restricting interchange across the Straits and lobbying for dual recognition or two Chinas in the international arena. It should be affirmed that the desire of Taiwan compatriots to run the affairs of the island as masters of their own house is reasonable and justified. This should by no means be construed as advocating "Taiwan independence". They are radically distinct from those handful of "Taiwan independence" protagonists who trumpet "independence" but vainly rely on foreign patronage in a vain attempt to detach Taiwan from China, which runs against the fundamental interests of the entire Chinese people including Taiwan compatriots. The Chinese Government is closely following the course of events and will never condone any maneuver for "Taiwan independence".

Certain foreign forces who do not want to see a reunified China have gone out of their way to meddle in China's internal affairs. They support the anti-Communist stance of the Taiwan authorities of rejecting peace talks and abet the secessionists on the island, thereby erecting barriers to China's peaceful reunification and seriously wounding the national feelings of the Chinese people.

The Chinese Government is convinced that Taiwan compatriots want national reunification and that this is also true with most of the political forces in or out of office in Taiwan. The people on both sides of the Straits will overcome all the barriers and stumbling blocks by their joint efforts and ensure a better development of relations across the Straits.

V. Several Questions Involving Taiwan in International Relations

As has been elucidated in the foregoing, there is only one China in the world, of which Taiwan is an inalienable part. The Government of the People's Republic of China has been recognized by the United Nations and throughout the world as the sole legal government representing the entire Chinese people. In the interest of safeguarding state sovereignty and realizing national reunification the Chinese Government has always stood firm on the principle of one China and ensured the interests of Taiwan compatriots in international relations involving Taiwan. The Chinese Government has no doubt that its position will be respected by all other governments and people.

The Chinese Government deems it necessary to reiterate its position and policy on the following matters.

1. Relations between Taiwan and countries maintaining diplomatic ties with China. All countries maintaining diplomatic relations with China have, in conformity with international law and the principle of one China, undertaken in formal agreement or understanding with the Chinese Government not to establish any ties of an official nature with Taiwan. According to international law, a sovereign state can only be represented by a single central government. As a part of China, Taiwan has no right to represent China in the international community, nor can it establish diplomatic ties or enter into relations of an official nature with foreign countries. Nevertheless, considering the needs of Taiwan's economic development and the practical interests of Taiwan compatriots, the Chinese Government has not objected to non-governmental economic or cultural exchanges between Taiwan and foreign countries.

In recent years the Taiwan authorities have vigorously launched a campaign of pragmatic diplomacy to cultivate official ties with countries having diplomatic relations with China in an attempt to push dual recognition and achieve the objective of creating a situation of two Chinas or one China, one Taiwan. The Chinese Government is firmly against this scheme.

It is noted that the overwhelming majority of the countries of the world cherish friendly relations with China and abide by their agreement or understanding with China on the issue of Taiwan. The Chinese Government appreciates this. On the other hand, it should be pointed out that, in disregard of their international credibility, certain countries have breached the undertaking made at the time of the establishment of diplomatic ties with the People s Republic of China by evolving official relations with Taiwan, thereby putting a spoke in the wheel of Chinas reunification. The Chinese Government sincerely hopes that the government in question will take measures to rectify the situation.

2. Relations between international organizations and Taiwan. The sovereignty of each state is an integral whole which is indivisible and unsharable. The Government of the People's Republic of China, as the sole legal government of China, has the right and obligation to exercise state sovereignty and represent the whole of China in international organizations. The Taiwan authorities' lobbying for a formula of 'one country, two seats" in international organizations whose membership is confined to sovereign states is a maneuver to create "two Chinas". The Chinese Government is firmly opposed to such an attempt. Its principled position fully conforms to the fundamental interests of the entire Chinese people including Taiwan compatriots and overseas Chinese. Only on the premise of adhering to the principle of one China and in the light of the nature and statutes of the international organizations concerned as well as the specific circumstances, can the Chinese Government consider the question of Taiwan's participation in the activities of such organizations and in a manner agreeable and acceptable to the Chinese Government.

All the specialized agencies and organizations of the United Nations system are inter-governmental organizations composed of sovereign states. After the restoration of the lawful rights of the People's Republic of China in the United Nations, all the specialized agencies and organizations of the U.N. system have formally adopted resolutions restoring to the People's Republic of China its lawful seat and expelling the "representatives" of the Taiwan authorities. Since then the issue of China's representation in the U.N. system has been resolved once and for all and Taiwan's re-entry is out of the question. However, it should be pointed out that recently some elements of the Taiwan authorities have been clamoring for "returning to the United Nations." Apparently this is an attempt to split state sovereignty, which is devoid of any legal or practical basis. The Chinese Government is convinced that all governments and organizations of the U.N. system will be alert to this scheme and refrain from doing anything prejudicial to China's sovereignty.

In principle, Taiwan is also ineligible for membership in other categories of inter-governmental organization. As to regional economic organizations such as the Asian Development Bank (ADB) and the Asia-Pacific Economic Cooperation (APEC), Taiwan's participation is subject to the terms of agreement or understanding reached between the Chinese Government and the parties concerned which explicitly prescribe that the People s Republic of China is a full member as a sovereign state whereas Taiwan may participate in the activities of those organizations only as a region of China under the designation of Taipei, China (in ADB) or Chinese Taipei (in APEC). This is only an *ad hoc* arrangement and cannot constitute a model applicable to other inter-governmental organizations or international gatherings.

As regards participation in non-governmental international organizations, the relevant bodies of the Peoples Republic of China may reach an agreement or understanding with the parties concerned so that China's national organizations would use the designation of China, while Taiwan organizations may participate under the designation of Taipei, China or Taiwan, China.

3. Aviation services between Taiwan and countries having diplomatic relations with China. Airspace is an inalienable part of a country's territory. The 1919 Paris Aviation Convention and the 1914

Chicago Convention affirm the principal of complete and exclusive sovereignty of each country over its airspace. Therefore, the opening of aviation services with Taiwan by any airlines, including privately-operated ones, of countries having diplomatic relations with China is a political issue affecting China's sovereignty and cannot be regarded as a non-political transaction. State-run airlines of countries having diplomatic relations with China certainly must not operate air services to Taiwan. Privately-operated airlines must seek China's consent through consultations between their government and the Chinese Government before they can start reciprocal air services with privately-operated airlines of Taiwan. As a matter of fact, according to the afore-said principle the Chinese government has consented to such services between privately-operated airlines of Britain, Germany, Canada, etc. and their counterparts in Taiwan.

As for countries which already had aviation services with Taiwan before the establishment of diplomatic relations with the People's Republic of China, they can negotiate with the Chinese Government to change the official nature of such services so as to be able to continue the operations as privately-run commercial transportation undertakings.

4. Arms sales to Taiwan by countries having diplomatic relations with China. The Chinese Government has always firmly opposed any country selling any type of arms or transferring production technology of the same to Taiwan. All countries maintaining diplomatic relations with China should abide by the principles of mutual respect or sovereignty and territorial integrity and non-interference in each other's internal affairs, and refrain from providing arms to Taiwan in any form or under any pretext. Failure to do so would be a breach of the norms of international relations and interference in China's internal affairs.

All countries, and especially big powers shouldering major responsibilities for world peace, are obligated to strictly abide by the guidelines laid down by the five permanent members of the U.N. Security Council to restrict the proliferation of conventional weapons so as to contribute to maintaining and promoting regional peace and security. However, at a time when relations across the Taiwan Straits are easing up, certain powers have seen fit to renege on their undertakings under international agreements and to flout the Chinese Government' s repeated strong representations by making arms sales to

Taiwan, thereby whipping up tension between the two sides of the Straits. This not only constitutes a serious threat to China's security and an obstacle to China's peaceful reunification, but also undermines peace and stability in Asia and the world at large. It stands to reason that the Chinese people should voice strong resentment against the conduct.

In international affairs the Chinese Government always pursues an independent foreign policy of peace and adheres to the Five Principles of mutual respect for sovereignty and territorial integrity, mutual non-aggression, non-interference in each others internal affairs. By the same taken it expects all other governments to refrain from undermining China's interests or interfering in China's internal affairs and to correctly handle their relations with Taiwan.

Conclusion

Reunification of the country embodies the fundamental interest of the Chinese nation.

After national reunification the two sides of the Taiwan Straits can pool their resources and make common cause in economic development and work towards China's resurgence. Numerous problems that have been besetting Taiwan would be judiciously resolved within the framework of one China. Taiwan compatriots will share the pride and glory of a great nation with their kith and kin from the other parts of the motherland.

The Taiwan question has long been a de-stabilizing factor in the Asia-Pacific region. Reunification of China will not only bolster the stability and development of the country itself, but also contribute to the further enhancement of the friendly relations and cooperation between China and other countries as well as to peace and development of the Asia-Pacific region and the world as a whole.

The Chinese Government is confident that it can count on the understanding and support of governments and people of all countries in the pursuit of its just cause of safeguarding its state sovereignty and territorial integrity.

Relations Across The Taiwan Straits

Mainland Affairs Council
The Executive Yuan
Republic of China

July 1994

I. Introduction

Since 1949, the Chinese people have lived in one of two societies with different ideologies and contrasting political, economic, and social systems on either side of the Taiwan Strait. In order to end this confrontation and estrangement between the two sides, and to achieve a strong and prosperous nation, the government of the Republic of China (ROC) has, since 1987, adopted concrete measures to promote cross-Strait exchanges. In February 1991, the "Guidelines for National Unification" were drawn up in an attempt to form a national consensus for the advance toward the unification of China. The ROC government has thus prepared a detailed explanation of relations between the two sides of the Taiwan Strait to give people at home and abroad a deeper understanding of its thinking, standpoint, and actions regarding national unification.

II. The Origins and Nature of the Division Between the Two Sides of the Taiwan Strait

In 1912, enlightened Chinese under the leadership of Dr. Sun Yat-sen established the Republic of China. In the early years of the Republic, China was extremely unstable, suffering from warlord strife within and the bullying and humiliation inflicted by the great powers from without. In an effort to save China and turn it into a strong and prosperous country, Sun Yat-sen had devised the Three Principles of the People which offered the correct answer to the question, "Whither China?" that had been asked ever since the Opium War.

In 1919, the Bolshevik Party in Russia established the Third International to promote world revolution, and neighboring China was the first country to feel its impact. In July 1921, a handful of leftist

93

intellectuals established the Chinese Communist Party (CCP), which acted as a branch of the Third International. From then on, communism began to spread on Chinese territory.

During the Northern Expedition [launched by the Nationalist government in 1926 to unite China], the CCP took advantage of the internal strife caused by the partition of the country under warlord regimes to foment large-scale uprisings, directing its efforts from then on toward seizing power through "armed struggle." In November 1931, the CCP established a "Chinese Soviet Republic," drawing up a "constitution" and organizing a "provisional central government." This act marked the beginning of the division of China in its recent history.

In 1937, the whole country rallied to resist the Japanese invaders, but the CCP took the opportunity to expand its bases and increase its military strength. After the Japanese defeat, the CCP forces launched an armed rebellion and swept across the entire Chinese mainland. In October 1949, the CCP established the People's Republic of China in Peking, and the ROC government transferred to Taipei. Since then, China has been a temporarily divided country under two separate governments on either side of the Taiwan Strait.

The division between the two sides of the Taiwan Strait is essentially the result of a struggle between the "China of the Three Principles of the People," which is founded on Chinese culture, and "Communist China," rooted in Marxism. This struggle between two contrasting political, economic, and social systems and two different ways of life is the essence of and the real reason for the division.

The reason why China cannot be unified today is not, as Peking would have it, that a section of the Taiwan population wishes to separate itself from China, neither is it due to the "interference of certain foreign forces." It is that the political system and level of economic development in mainland China, and its frequent large-scale and violent power struggles, have destroyed people's confidence in the CCP regime. This is why the ROC government has repeatedly insisted that "there is only a China problem, not a Taiwan problem."

III. The Development of Cross-Strait Relations

For a long period of time, the CCP regime sought to "liberate" Taiwan by force. Beginning in 1949, it launched a series of military attacks in an effort to complete unification by force. After the Peking regime failed in its attempt to take Kinmen (Quemoy) by force, mainland China was struck by a series of difficulties in its domestic affairs and foreign relations, so apart from calling loudly for "peaceful liberation," Peking lacked the resources to undertake any further military action.

In 1979, on account of Washington's establishing diplomatic relations with Peking and breaking off official ties with the Republic of China, an important change took place in Peking's strategy toward the ROC. In order to create an illusion of peace in the international arena, the CCP dropped references to "liberation" in propaganda aimed at Taiwan, replacing them with "peaceful unification." But though it claims to be pursuing "peaceful unification," Peking has refused to give up the option of using force to solve the unification problem.

The ROC government has always believed that a change of system in mainland China is crucial to solving the China problem. Therefore, in April 1981, the ruling Kuomintang put out a call for the "unification of China under the Three Principles of the People." This proposal immediately became the core of the ROC government's mainland policy. The ROC government's chief reason for advocating unification under the Three Principles of the People" was that Marxism/Leninism had failed utterly in practice while the Three Principles had proved better suited to the conditions of China and better able to solve the "China problem."

In the 1980s, the pace of economic liberalization, social pluralization, and political democratization speeded up in Taiwan. Then, with the lifting of martial law, the government adopted a more open policy toward mainland China. From this time on, cross Strait relations progressed from a state of complete estrangement toward people-to-people exchanges.

On April 30, 1991, President Lee Tenghui announced that the period of mobilization for the suppression of communist rebellion would be terminated at midnight on May 1, and in accordance with a resolution passed by the National Assembly, he also announced that the "temporary provisions" of the Constitution in force during the mobilization period would be annulled simultaneously.

This announcement had two important implications. First of all, it demonstrated that the ROC government had formally and unilaterally renounced use of force as a means of national unification. Secondly, it showed that the ROC government would no longer compete with Peking for the "right to represent China" in the international arena. The government held that "there is only one China," but "Taiwan and the mainland are both parts of China," and "the Peking regime is not equivalent to China." Prior to unification, these two parts of China should have the right to participate alongside each other in the international community.

It is an incontrovertible historical fact that the Republic of China has been an independent sovereign state since its establishment in 1912. However, relations between the two sides of the Taiwan Strait are not those between two separate countries, neither are they purely domestic in nature. In order to ensure that cross-Strait relations develop toward friendly interaction, the ROC government has formulated the concept of a "political entity" to serve as the basis of interaction between the two sides. Only when we set aside the "sovereignty dispute" will we untangle the knots that have bound us for the past forty years or more and progress smoothly toward unification. The concept of a "political entity" is the key to loosening those knots.

The ROC government believes that China, as it is traditionally defined, is currently divided into two political entities: a free and democratic Taiwan, and mainland China which practices a socialist system. In Peking's eyes, the "one country" is the "People's Republic of China," and Taiwan under the jurisdiction of the Republic of China can only be a "special administrative region" under Peking's rule. Although Peking may permit it to enjoy a "high degree of autonomy" within certain limitations, it must not violate the PRC "constitution" or the decrees of the "central government." It is obvious that the purpose of "one country, two systems" is to make the Republic of China surrender completely to Peking, and to make the people of Taiwan give up their free and democratic system. For this reason it is both absolutely unacceptable and unworkable.

The ROC government is firm in its advocacy of "one China," and it is opposed to "two Chinas" or "one China, one Taiwan." But at the same time, given that the division between the two sides of the Taiwan Strait is a longstanding political fact, the ROC government also holds that the two sides should be fully aware that each has jurisdiction over its respective territory and that they should coexist as two legal entities in the international arena. As for their relationship with each other, it is that of two separate areas of one China and is therefore "domestic" or "Chinese" in nature. This position is extremely pragmatic. These proposals are quite different from either "two Chinas" or "one China, one Taiwan."

In the course of cross-Strait exchanges, Peking should dismiss any misgivings it has concerning the ROC government's determination to achieve unification. What the Peking authorities should give urgent consideration to is how, given the fact that the country is divided under two separate governments, we can actively create favorable conditions for unification and gradually bring the "two political entities" together to form "one China."

In the period prior to peaceful unification, the Republic of China proposes that cross-Strait relations be handled according to the principles of reason, peace, parity, and reciprocity.

We should always think rationally when we are handling cross-Strait affairs. And for a divided country, the principles of peace, parity, and reciprocity are the best expressions of reason. The unification of Germany, which was carried out according to the rational principles of equal treatment, reciprocal contacts, and the peaceful resolution of disputes, is an example from which we would do well to learn.

The principle of peace is fundamental to the handling of cross-Strait relations. Cross Strait interaction is no longer a game which one side can win outright, it is a "win-win" contest in which both sides must be prepared to compromise and each can further its own interests. To seek "territorial unification" through armed force is a shallow, parochial distortion of the true meaning of nationalism; an enduring, all-embracing form of nationalism can only be expressed in a "unification of systems" through democracy, freedom, and equitable prosperity.

Our third principle is parity, which means that Chinese people in both Taiwan and the mainland should be able to enjoy the same degree of dignity and respect. The ROC government believes that both current people-to-people exchanges and future government-to-government talks should be conducted according to the principle of respect for each other's people and government, and neither side should try to humiliate the other.

Reciprocity is the fourth principle underlying our policy toward mainland China. Exchanges between the two sides of the Taiwan Strait should serve the interests of both parties; relations should always be "win-win" rather than "zero sum." Only when we have reciprocal exchanges will we be able to establish mutual trust and mutual understanding, and only then can relations be broad-based and long-lasting, and make steady progress. Reciprocal actions cannot be considered in a one-sided or partial way; they must take into consideration both parties and the situation as a whole.

IV. Domestic and External Factors Affecting Cross-Strait Relations

The various factors influencing relations between the two sides of the Taiwan Strait may be roughly divided into three categories: international factors, factors originating in mainland China, and factors within Taiwan itself.

As far as international factors are concerned, by the 1990s, communism had proved itself to be unacceptable, and this was the chief reason for the disintegration of the Soviet Union and the collapse of communism in Eastern Europe. In the post-Cold War situation, the international community began to take a more reasonable attitude toward the division of China under two separate governments on either side of the Taiwan Strait, to realize that the Republic of China could play a role in the mainland's reform and opening up process, and to recognize the importance of security in the Taiwan Strait to the stability of Asia and the economic development of the Asia-Pacific region. In addition, the growing importance of economic interdependence in international relations has also been beneficial to cross-Strait detente.

International trends toward integration and division are also having an impact on relations between the two sides of the Taiwan Strait. In Taiwan, the passing of the "Guidelines for National Unification" was an affirmation of the trend toward integration, while on the other hand, proposals for Taiwan independence have been stimulated by the separatist trend. Subjectively speaking, the ROC government believes that we should work toward integration, but in objective terms, the degree of acceptance which these two trends enjoy among the people of Taiwan will depend on the future development of relations between the two sides of the Taiwan Strait.

As for the situation on the Chinese mainland and the CCP regime's policy toward Taiwan, although the CCP has decided to establish a "Chinese-style socialist market economy," politically it is still upholding the "four cardinal principles" which underpin the one-party dictatorship. The constant economic and financial crises that mainland China has suffered in recent years, the widening gap between rich and poor, and the appearance of all kinds of social problems are all results of this policy of "political leftism and economic rightism." In the future, domestic political trends in mainland China will have an impact on the Taiwan people's attitude to unification.

The CCP leaders have never relinquished the threat of using force against Taiwan. In addition, Peking has always sought to prevent the Republic of China from participating in international activities. But hostile actions such as these will not only fail to rupture the Republic of China's foreign relations, they will actually stir up more hatred for the Peking regime in Taiwan and obstruct the process of national unification.

Concerning the future political and economic development of Taiwan, it might be said that the Republic of China on Taiwan has undergone a "quiet revolution" in recent years. Economically and politically, it has established the first prosperous and democratic society in China's history, according respect for human rights and the rule of law. After this accumulation of economic strength and social and cultural vitality had found its release through democratization and liberalization, it had an impact in two directions: toward the outside world in the shape of the ROC's "pragmatic diplomacy," and toward mainland China where it has acted as a catalyst for the expansion of all kinds of people-to-people exchanges.

It is a pity that the CCP authorities have not only failed to understand this cause and effect relationship, they actually ridicule or attack Taiwan's democratization process and interfere unreasonably with the Republic of China's external relations. This kind of behavior fails to take into account political and economic development trends in Taiwan in recent years and pays no regard whatsoever to the real wishes and welfare of the people of Taiwan. If it continues, it will inevitably have a negative impact on the unification of China and normal exchanges between the two sides of the Strait.

Taiwan is already a democratic, pluralistic society. Opposition members occupy a considerable number of seats in the Legislative Yuan (Parliament), and their opinions inevitably have an influence on the government's mainland policy. Where national identity and cross-Strait relations are concerned, the ruling party and the opposition differ quite considerably. But although the various parties may have different opinions concerning mainland policy, their ultimate purpose is to enhance the welfare of the people of Taiwan. They always have to give careful consideration as to the impact of their proposals on the security and welfare of Taiwan's 21 million people.

V. Conclusion

The division of China under two separate governments is a great misfortune for the Chinese people. We call on the CCP to further promote its economic reforms and carry out all-round political reform, as this alone can deliver our mainland compatriots from poverty and want and allow them to live lives *of* humanity and dignity. We also call on the Peking regime to face up to the fact that China is a divided country under two separate governments, and to promote the development of cross-Strait relations according to the principles of reason, peace, parity, and reciprocity. This is the only way we can create an opportunity for the peaceful unification of China.

We believe that the Chinese people are absolutely against either military threats or the devastation of war. Anyone who resorts to arms in the name of unification will be condemned by history.

The real significance of unification lies not only in the achievement of a strong and prosperous country and the long-term development of the Chinese nation, it also lies in enabling the Chinese people to enjoy democracy, freedom, and equitable prosperity. If we cannot achieve this, unification will be completely meaningless and worthless.

Looking back over the past and forward to the future, the ROC government will continue to adhere to its present stance and make every effort to promote cross-Strait relations to ensure the favorable development of interaction between the two sides. We are confident that the wisdom and efforts of the entire people will enable us to create a new situation, speed up political, economic, and social modernization in mainland China, and eventually complete the sacred mission of unifying China under democracy, freedom, and equitable prosperity.

I. Introduction

Many countries throughout history have experienced periods of division and reunification, and the history of China is also one of periodic partition and unity. Modern China has been unable to escape this historical cycle. Since 1949, the Chinese people have lived in one of two societies on either side of the Taiwan Strait with different ideologies and political, economic, and social systems.

In order to end this confrontation and estrangement between the two sides of the Taiwan Strait and to achieve a strong and prosperous nation, the government of the Republic of China (ROC) has, since 1987, adopted concrete measures to promote social, cultural, and economic exchanges between the two sides of the Strait in a forward-looking, pragmatic, active, and moderate way. In February 1991, the ROC government drew upon the insight of people inside and outside the ruling party in drawing up the "Guidelines for National Unification," part of an attempt to form a national consensus for the advance toward unification.

However, creating the conditions for unification requires sincere cooperation between the two sides of the Strait. And completing the momentous task of unification is even more dependent on the joint efforts of the two sides.

For this reason, the ROC government believes that it must present a detailed and exhaustive explication of relations between the two sides of the Taiwan Strait, in the hope that this will enable people at home and abroad to gain a thorough understanding of the government's thinking, position, and actions regarding the issue of national unification. In this way we may pool our wisdom and efforts and work together to create a democratic, free, and prosperous China.

II. The Origins and Nature of the Division Between the Two Sides of the Taiwan Strait

The Founding of the Republic of China

After the Opium War in the mid-nineteenth century, enlightened Chinese began to perceive the evils of despotism. They were convinced that if China failed to become independent and strong, if it did not introduce reforms and establish a democratic republic, it would be impossible to reverse its decline. Then in 1912, under the leadership of Dr. Sun Yat-sen and thanks to the self-sacrificing struggle of the revolutionaries, Asia's first democratic republic--the Republic of China -was born.

In the early years of the Republic, China was extremely unstable, suffering from warlord strife within and the bullying and humiliation inflicted by the great powers from without. In an effort to save China and make it strong and prosperous, Dr. Sun Yatsen had combined the finest elements of Chinese and Western thinking into the Three Principles of the People. His Principle of Nationalism was aimed at recovering China's independence and autonomy; his Principle of People's Rights is interpreted as political democracy; and the Principle of the People's Livelihood seeks to achieve equitable prosperity and to avoid the ills of both capitalism and communism, thus combining political and social revolution. The Three Principles of the People offered the correct answer to the question, "Whither China?" that had been asked ever since the Opium War.

The Birth and Development of Communism in China

At that time, however, the situation in China and the world at large provided an opportunity for the development of communism. During the October Revolution of 1917, the Bolsheviks under Lenin seized power in Russia. Soon after, they established the Third International as a means of promoting world revolution, and neighboring China was the first country to feel its impact. The year 1919 saw the outbreak in Peking of the May Fourth Movement, which had a profound and far reaching influence. The doctrine of "out-and-out Westernization," which made an appearance during the May Fourth period, provided an opening for the introduction of Marxism to China. In July 1921, a handful of leftist intellectuals established the Chinese Communist Party (CCP), which acted as a branch of the Third International. From then on, communism began to spread on Chinese territory, and   in 1924, the Kuomintang (KMT, or the Nationalist Party), under Soviet influence, adopted a policy of "allying with Russia and accommodating the communists," which allowed the CCP to develop and become strong within the ranks of the KMT.

During the Northern Expedition [launched by the Nationalist government in 1926 to unite China], the CCP took advantage of the internal strife caused by the partition of the country under warlord regimes to foment large-scale peasant uprisings in Nanchang, Changsha, Hailufeng, and Canton, directing its efforts from then on toward seizing power through "armed struggle." In November 1931, the CCP established a "Chinese Soviet Republic" in Juichin, Kiangsi Province, drawing up a "constitution" and organizing a "provisional central government." By using the term "soviet" in the title of its government, the CCP was demonstrating that it was an offspring of Moscow, the "proletarian motherland." This act also marked the beginning of the division of China once again.

After the Marco Polo Bridge incident of 1937, the whole country rallied to resist the Japanese invaders. During this period, the CCP forces adopted the tactic of "devoting one-tenth of their efforts to resisting the Japanese, two-tenths to coping with the Nationalist central government, and seven-tenths to building up their own strength," expanding their bases and increasing their firepower. After the Japanese defeat, the CCP was able to take advantage of the Chinese people's exhaustion to launch an armed rebellion and sweep across the entire Chinese mainland. In October 1949, the CCP established the People's Republic of China in Peking, and the ROC government transferred from Nanking to Canton, and thence to Taipei. Since then, China has been a temporarily divided country under two separate governments on either side of the Taiwan Strait.

A Struggle between Systems: The Essence of China's Division

In traditional China, periods of partition were attributable to struggles for power; the division of the country indicated a division of ruling power and jurisdiction, it had nothing to do with ideology. Division of the kind that exists now between the two sides of the Taiwan Strait is unprecedented in Chinese history. On the surface, it seems to result from the struggle for power between two political parties during the Chinese Civil War. But it stems essentially from the influence of the international political situation and an alien ideology, which eventually took the form of a struggle between the "China of the Three Principles of the People," which is founded on Chinese culture, and "Communist China," rooted in Marxism. It is also a struggle between two contrasting political, economic, and social systems and two different ways of life. In particular, after four decades of division under two different systems, there is an obvious disparity in economic and social development between the two sides. This is a concrete manifestation of the struggle over the question, "Whither China?" that is the essence of the division between the two sides of the Taiwan

Strait and the real reason why China is divided. If this fundamental difference is not removed, it will be extremely difficult for China to move from division to unity.

The fundamental reason why China cannot be unified is not, as Peking would have it, that a section of the Taiwan population wishes to separate itself from China, neither is it due to the "interference of certain foreign forces." It is that the political system and level of economic development in mainland China, and its frequent large-scale and violent power struggles, have destroyed people's confidence in the CCP regime. When mainland China's young people, who have grown up under communism, are doing their best to get out of the country, or refusing to return once they have left, or being refused permission to return when they wish to; when thousands of mainland Chinese are illegally emigrating; when none of the most ardent Chinese supporters of unification in Taiwan and overseas are willing to settle in mainland China; and when Peking will not countenance even the minimum degree of democracy in Hong Kong, how can the CCP regime blame us for hesitating over unification? If there was freedom and democracy in mainland China and if its economy came up to modern standards, who among the Chinese would not wish to see their country united? How could foreigners interfere? The crux of the problem thus lies with no one else but the CCP regime itself. This is why the ROC government has repeatedly insisted that "there is no Taiwan problem, only a China problem."

III. The Development of Cross-Strait Relations

The Evolution of Peking's Taiwan Policy

For a long period of time, the Peking regime sought to "liberate" Taiwan by force. In October 1949, Peking launched an amphibious attack on the island of Kinmen (Quemoy), but its forces were heavily defeated. Then in September 1954, the CCP armed forces began their bombardment of Kinmen, sparking off a crisis in the Taiwan Strait. In January 1955, they carried out a bloody attack on Ikiangshan Island and occupied the Tachen Islands. In 1958 came the "August 23 bombardment" of Kinmen, an event that sent shockwaves around the world. One might say that up to the time of the August 23 attack, Peking was seeking to complete the task of unification by force, though it would at the same time occasionally call for the "peaceful liberation of Taiwan."

After the failure of the attempt to take Kinmen by force, mainland China was struck by a series of disasters. First came the natural and man-made calamities that stemmed from the "three red banners" program, then the split with Moscow resulted in the withdrawal of all Soviet aid. With the outbreak of the Cultural Revolution in 1966, the mainland was brought even nearer to the brink of collapse. In addition, the regime experienced armed border clashes with India and the Soviet Union. Beset by difficulties within and without, Peking lacked the resources to undertake any further military action with regard to Taiwan, apart from calling loudly for "peaceful liberation." As Peking-Moscow relations deteriorated and the entire communist camp was split, the United States--deeply antagonistic toward the Soviet Union and eager to extricate itself from the Vietnam War--began to align itself with Peking against the Soviets. Strategic considerations brought about an alleviation of tension between Washington and Peking, causing the focus of the conflict between Taiwan and mainland China to shift outward from the Taiwan Strait into the international arena. Now, the competition between the two sides took the form of attempts at international isolation and counter-isolation.

In 1979, the United States established diplomatic relations with the CCP regime and broke off official ties with the Republic of China. No longer afraid that Washington would intervene directly in relations between the two sides of the Strait, Peking made an important change in its strategy toward the ROC. In order to create an impression of peace in the international arena that would facilitate the promotion of its economic reform and opening-up program, Peking launched a "smiling offensive." In propaganda aimed at Taiwan, the CCP dropped references to "liberation," replacing them with "peaceful unification." On January 1, 1979, the standing committee of mainland China's National People's Congress (NPC) issued a "letter to Taiwan compatriots" which called for the "peaceful unification of the motherland" and the establishment of the "three links and four exchanges." At the same time, Peking stopped its bombardment of Kinmen and Matsu. In September 1981, the chairman of the NPC standing committee, Yeh Chien-ying, issued a nine-point proposal "concerning the return of Taiwan to the motherland and the realization of peaceful unification." Then in 1984, Teng Hsiao-p'ing put forward the "one country, two systems" unification formula. Though all these declarations were issued in the name of "peaceful unification," to this day the Chinese Communists have refused to give up the option of using force to solve the unification problem.

The ROC Government's Efforts to Promote Cross-Strait Relations

The ROC government has always believed that a change of system in mainland China is crucial to solving the China problem. Therefore, at its twelfth national congress in April 1981, the ruling Kuomintang put out a call for the "unification of China under the Three Principles of the People," claiming that the only way to unify China was to implement the Three Principles throughout the entire country. These calls became the central theme of the Republic of China's mainland policy. In other words, the dispute between the two sides of the Strait hinged on whether a free and democratic China or a China under communist dictatorship best fulfilled the aspirations of the Chinese people and served the interests of the world as a whole. The ROC government's chief reason for advocating "unification under the Three Principles of the People" was that the practice of these two contrasting systems over the past three decades or more, both on the two sides of the Strait and in the world at large, had resulted in the utter defeat of Marxism-Leninism, while the Three Principles had proved better suited to the conditions of China and therefore able to solve the "China problem." Political movements launched under the communist system, such as land reform, the "hundred flowers," the "three red banners," and the Cultural Revolution, had cost the Chinese people dearly, and even the CCP itself was now describing them as "catastrophes." In Taiwan, however, the ROC government had implemented Sun Yatsen's Three Principles of the People and had promoted economic development and political reform in a moderate and gradual manner, creating prosperity and democracy on a scale unprecedented in Chinese history.

In the 1980s, the pace of economic liberalization, social pluralization, and political democratization was stepped up in Taiwan, causing the Republic of China to undergo a rapid transformation. Then, with the lifting of martial law, the government adopted a series of more open policies toward mainland China. On November 2, 1987, President Chiang Ching-kuo, inspired by traditional moral principles and humanitarian considerations, allowed Taiwan residents to visit their relatives on the mainland, ending nearly four decades of estrangement and marking a turning-point in relations between the two sides of the Taiwan Strait. From this time on, cross-Strait relations progressed from a state of complete estrangement toward people-to-people exchanges.

In May 1990, during his inaugural address after he was sworn in as the eighth president of the ROC, President Lee Teng-hui made the following announcement:

> If the Chinese communist authorities can recognize the overall world trend and the common hope of all Chinese, implement political democracy and a free economic system, renounce the use of military force in the Taiwan Strait, and not interfere with our development of foreign relations on the basis of a one-China policy, we would be willing, on a basis of equality, to establish channels of communication, and completely open up academic, cultural, economic, trade, scientific, and technological exchange, to lay a foundation of mutual respect, peace, and prosperity.

President Lee also said that he hoped that "the period of mobilization for the suppression of communist rebellion" could be terminated, in accordance with the law, as quickly as possible. These solemn proclamations laid an important foundation for friendly interaction between the two sides of the Taiwan Strait.

In an effort to form a national consensus on various problems, the government convened a National Affairs Conference (NAC) in June 1990, during which it was agreed that the governments on the two sides of the Strait were both "political entities with de facto authority." The participants also called for a "relaxation of functional exchanges and an uncompromising attitude toward political negotiations" in relations between the two sides, and for relations to be handled by a special government agency and an authorized private intermediary body. In addition, the NAC recommended that after the termination of "the period of mobilization for the suppression of communist rebellion," the Peking regime should be defined as a "confrontational competitive regime," and it also requested that the government draw up a cross-Strait relations law to regulate exchanges between the two sides.

In October 1990, President Lee invited individuals from the ruling and opposition parties and other figures outside politics to sit on a National Unification Council (NUC), charged with drawing up the "Guidelines for National Unification" which would define the goals for different phases of the ROC's future mainland China policy and constitute a long range blueprint for national unification. In January 1991, the Executive Yuan (ROC Cabinet) set up the ministry-level Mainland Affairs Council to take charge of planning and handling mainland affairs on behalf of the government. The following month, the Straits Exchange Foundation (SEF) was established and authorized by the government to handle practical issues arising from cross-Strait relations that touched on government authority. The "Guidelines for National Unification," which serve as the guiding principles for relations across the Taiwan Strait, were passed by the Executive Yuan in March that year. Then on April 30, President Lee announced that the "period of mobilization" would be terminated at midnight on May 1, and in accordance with a resolution passed by the National Assembly, he also announced that the "temporary provisions" of the Constitution in force during the mobilization period would be annulled simultaneously.   Constitutionally speaking, this meant that the Peking regime was no longer regarded as a rebel organization. This was the Republic of China's first major gesture of goodwill toward the Peking regime since the promulgation of the "Guidelines for National Unification."

This announcement had two important implications for cross- Strait relations. First of all, it demonstrated that the ROC government had formally and unilaterally renounced military force as a means of national unification.

Secondly, it showed that the ROC government would no longer compete for the "right to represent China" in the international arena. The government held that there was "only one China," but "Taiwan and the mainland were both parts of China," and "the Peking regime was not equivalent to China." Prior to unification, China was ruled by two separate governments which should have the right to participate alongside each other in the international community.

In July 1992, the ROC Legislative Yuan (Parliament) passed the "Statute Governing Relations Between the People of Taiwan and the Mainland Areas," which took effect on September 18 that year. This statute provided a legal basis for the government's handling of cross-Strait relations.

Increasingly frequent exchanges between the two sides of the Taiwan Strait were giving rise to quite a few problems, and the need to establish systematic channels for solving disputes was becoming ever more urgent. In September 1990, the Red Cross organizations on the two sides of the Strait signed the first cross-Strait agreement between non-official bodies--the Kinmen Agreement--which was designed to handle the return of the large numbers of illegal immigrants from mainland China. Originally, the two sides had agreed that the mainland side would fetch the migrants and return them to their places of origin within twenty days of receiving notification from Taiwan. But the mainland side found various excuses for delaying, causing the nearly 30,000 illegal migrants who had crossed the Strait in the past few years to spend an average of 113 days in detention in Taiwan. It was to solve such routine problems arising from cross-Strait exchanges that the SEF and its mainland Chinese counterpart, the Association for Relations Across the Taiwan Straits (ARATS), met to exchange opinions on various occasions in Peking and Hong Kong. The two organizations also agreed that in order to establish effective channels for liaison, their respective chairmen would hold talks in Singapore in April 1993. During the talks, Koo Chen-fu and Wang Daohan formally signed four agreements: the "Agreement on Document Authentication," the Agreement on Tracing of and Compensation for Lost Registered Mail," the "Agreement on the Establishment of Systematic Liaison and Communication Channels between the SEF and the ARATS," and the "Koo-Wang Talks Joint Agreement." These laid a foundation for future talks on routine matters and systematic interaction between the two sides of the Strait. In accordance with these agreements, the SEF and ARATS have since held several rounds of follow-up talks, and continued to discuss problems arising from cross-Strait exchanges.

The ROC Government's Conception of Cross-Strait Relations

Apart from demonstrating that after more than forty years of confrontation the two sides now intend to solve their disputes through negotiation, these talks also show that they mean to use the experience gathered through talks on routine issues to prepare the ground for future contacts and negotiations of a political nature. However, these talks have given rise to a number of disputes, on such subjects as the meaning of the term "one China," and the problem of legal jurisdiction. Problems like these affect the orientation of cross-Strait relations and if they are not solved will influence their development.

That the Republic of China has been an independent sovereign state since its establishment in 1912 is an incontrovertible historical fact. However, relations between the two sides of the Taiwan Strait are not those between two separate countries, neither are they purely domestic in nature. In order to ensure that cross-Strait relations develop toward friendly interaction, the ROC government has formulated the concept of a "political entity" to serve as the basis of interaction between the two sides. The meaning of the term "political entity" is quite broad; it can be applied to a state, a government, or a political organization. Only when the two sides of the Taiwan Strait set aside the "sovereignty dispute" for the time being will we untangle the knots that have bound us for the past forty years or more and progress smoothly toward unification. The concept of a "political entity" will help us loosen those knots.

The "Guidelines for National Unification" suggest the idea of "one China, two equal political entities" as a way of defining the future development of cross-Strait relations. This idea comprises the following:

1. The existence of the Republic of China is a simple reality that cannot be denied.
2. "One China" refers to China as a historical, geographical, cultural, and racial entity.
3. The division of China under two separate governments on either side of the Taiwan Strait is a temporary, transitional phenomenon in Chinese history, and the joint efforts of the two sides will inevitably put China once again on the road to unification. Therefore, in the process of seeking unification, the two sides may first eradicate mutual hostility through routine people-to-people exchanges and then proceed to create the conditions for unification. The two sides should also respect, rather than exclude, each other in the international arena, and

should renounce armed force as a means for achieving unification.

4. Room should be left for future political negotiations. It is precisely because China is divided into two political entities that we must bring about its unification through exchanges and negotiations. The "Guidelines for National Unification" clearly stipulate that in the long-term phase of consultation for unification, the two sides will establish a consultative body and complete the plans for unification through negotiation.

The ROC Government's Rejection of "One Country, Two Systems"

The Republic of China's understanding of the current temporary division of China between the two sides of the Taiwan Strait is completely different from Peking's idea of "one country, two systems." We believe that China, as it is traditionally defined, is currently divided into two political entities: mainland China which practices socialism, and a free and democratic Taiwan. In Peking's eyes, the "one country" is the "People's Republic of China," and Taiwan under the jurisdiction of the Republic of China can only be a "special administrative region" under Peking's rule. Although Peking may permit it to enjoy a "high degree of autonomy" within certain limitations, it must not violate the PRC "constitution" or the decrees of the "central government." This takes no account whatsoever of the existence of the Republic of China and indeed amounts to nothing more than annexing Taiwan, Penghu, Kinmen, and Matsu in the name of unifying China. The status of Peking's "two systems" is different too, with socialism as practiced in mainland China acting as the main force and capitalism as practiced in Taiwan only allowed to play a supplementary role, and only permitted to exist during a transitional period. The Peking authorities believe that they alone have the right to define and interpret the content and time-frame of the "two systems." Thus, the "two systems" is an expedient measure deriving from Peking's domination. In essence, the relationship between the two systems is one of principal and subordinate: one system represents the center and the other the local authority. Under this arrangement, Taiwan will be forced to give up its freedom and democracy, and to accept entirely the system prescribed by the CCP regime. It is obvious that the purpose of "one country, two systems" is to make the Republic of China surrender completely to Peking and the people of Taiwan abandon their free and democratic system. For this reason it is both unworkable and absolutely unacceptable to us.

The ROC government believes that from the point of view of political reality, China is at present temporarily divided into two areas under two essentially equal political entities, the government of the Republic of China and the Peking regime. Although these two entities differ in terms of the extent of their jurisdiction, their population, and the systems they implement, they should treat each other equally in the course of their interaction. And in the areas over which they have jurisdiction, each should have exclusive rights; neither entity should be able to exercise its rule in the territory of the other, nor should one force its will on the other in the name of sovereignty.

The ROC Government's Adherence to the Goal of the Unification

The ROC government is firm in its advocacy of "one China," and it is opposed to "two Chinas" or "one China, one Taiwan." But at the same time, given that the division between the two sides of the Taiwan Strait is a historical and political fact, the ROC government also holds that the two sides should be fully aware that each has jurisdiction over its respective territory and that they should coexist as two legal entities in the international arena. As for their relationship with each other, it is that of two separate areas of one China and is therefore "domestic" or "Chinese" in nature. This position is extremely pragmatic. These proposals are quite different from either "two Chinas" or "one China, one Taiwan."

By adopting "one China, two equal political entities" as the framework for cross-Strait relations, the ROC government hopes that relations will develop in a peaceful, pragmatic, and rational direction. The Peking authorities should realize that this is the best way to promote the unification of China. In the course of cross-Strait exchanges, Peking should dismiss any misgivings it has concerning the ROC government's determination to achieve unification. What the Peking authorities should give urgent consideration to is how, given the fact that the country is divided under two separate governments, we can actively create conditions favorable to unification and gradually bring the two "political entities" together to form "one

China." Furthermore, both sides of the Taiwan Strait should adopt moderate unification policies; it is inappropriate to be too impatient as more haste will only mean less speed. As long as both sides are sincere and determined, unification will surely be achieved in the end. Meanwhile, there is no point in the Chinese seeking unification for its own sake; unification should take place under a reasonable and sound political, economic, and social system and way of life. Therefore, we propose that the two sides of the Taiwan Strait should put all their efforts into establishing a united China that is democratic, free, and equitably prosperous. Once the ideological, political, economic, and social gap between the two sides is bridged as a result of our joint efforts, the unification of China will come naturally.

For the time being, the two sides of the Taiwan Strait should intensify their exchanges and resolve conflicts by means of negotiations on functional matters. Only when a certain amount of experience has been accumulated and certain successes achieved through such negotiations will it be possible for the two sides to start political contacts and talks. In other words, as functional negotiations become more frequent, and more and more agreements are signed, there will be more opportunity for political contacts and negotiations. The ROC government is pursuing its mainland policy in an orderly and gradual fashion in accordance with the "Guidelines for National Unification," and we hope that this will evoke a positive and well-intentioned response from the Peking authorities. In that way, the two sides of the Taiwan Strait may achieve friendly interaction which will create conditions favorable to the peaceful and democratic unification of China.

The ROC Government's Principles for Handling Cross-Strait Relations

In the period prior to peaceful unification, the Republic of China proposes that cross-Strait relations be handled according to the principles of reason, peace, parity, and reciprocity.

We should always think rationally when we are handling cross-Strait affairs. And for a divided country, the principles of peace, parity, and reciprocity are the best expressions of reason. The unification of Germany, for example, was carried out according to the rational principles of equal treatment, reciprocal contacts, and the peaceful resolution of disputes, while the way in which the European Union has rationally handled its progress from a customs union to a single market, and then to one big European family is another example we could learn from. If national unification is not handled in a rational way, the result will be another round of civil strife and chaos, with people being uprooted from their homes. The painful examples of Vietnam, and recently Yugoslavia, should serve as a warning to the two sides of the Taiwan Strait.

The principle of peace is fundamental to the handling of cross-Strait relations. From what President Lee Teng-hui has said on many occasions, it is clear that he rejects the option of using armed force to resolve the problem of unification. His reasons for doing so are threefold. First of all, the trend in international affairs is toward negotiation rather than confrontation, and all countries should as far as possible avoid recourse to armed force in solving their conflicts. Secondly, cross-Strait interaction is no longer a game which one side can win outright, it is a "win-win" contest in which both sides must be prepared to compromise and both can further their own interests. Thirdly, the best interests of the Chinese people can only be served by rejecting the option of armed force. Therefore, only when the Peking authorities choose an appropriate moment to announce that they reject the option of unification by force will a friendly atmosphere in which to conduct cross-Strait relations be created. To seek "territorial unification" through armed force is a shallow, parochial distortion of the true meaning of nationalism; an enduring, all embracing form of nationalism can only be expressed in a "unification of systems" through democracy, freedom, and equitable prosperity. Peking has always used the excuse that the existence of "forces for Taiwan independence" and "foreign interference" prevent it from renouncing the option of using force against Taiwan. But advocates of Taiwan independence represent only a minority of the population, and it is surely senseless to bully the majority which identifies with the Chinese nation and Chinese culture just to attack that minority. And to claim to be resisting "foreign interference" while in reality to be directly threatening the security of the entire population of Taiwan is even more inconsistent.

Our third principle is parity, which means that Chinese people in both Taiwan and the mainland should be able to enjoy the same degree of dignity and respect. The ROC government believes that both the current people-to-people exchanges and future government-to-government talks should be conducted according to the principle of mutual respect for each other's people and government, and neither side should try to humiliate the other. For example, the Peking authorities are opposed to the use of "Republic of China, ROC government," or "national" by any group from Taiwan visiting the mainland, and they will unilaterally change such titles to "Taiwan." They are also opposed to any government-to-government signing of agreements concerning cross-Strait exchanges, and they refuse to recognize that our government has any legal jurisdiction. In addition, Peking always forces us to change our name to "Chinese Taipei" when we take part in any international organizations or activities, in an attempt to downgrade the Republic of China's international standing. Actually, such actions could only have the effect of generating a high tide of separatist feeling in Taiwan.

Reciprocity is the fourth principle underlying our policy toward mainland China. Exchanges between the two sides of the Taiwan Strait should serve the interests of both parties; relations should always be "win-win" rather than "zero sum." Only when exchanges are conducted on a reciprocal basis will we be able to establish mutual trust and mutual understanding, and only then can relations be broad-based and long-lasting, and make steady progress. Reciprocal actions cannot be considered in a one-sided or partial way, they must take into consideration both parties and the situation as a-whole. Since the two sides have different conceptions of exchanges, they have different opinions regarding their scope and speed. In economic exchanges and trade, for example, although the Peking authorities claim that no one is trying to "swallow up" anyone else, they have actually adopted a tactic of "the strong devouring the weak," and they hold that economic exchanges should be elevated to a strategic level so as to "tie up Taiwan." The ROC government, on the other hand, holds that cross-Strait economic exchanges should be developed steadily and gradually according to the principles of complementarily and mutual benefit. In other words, Peking hopes to use cross-Strait economic exchanges to achieve its goal of annexing Taiwan as quickly as possible, whereas the ROC government hopes that such exchanges will promote mutual understanding, dispel hostility, and narrow the gap between the people on the two sides of the Strait, so that their relations will become complementary and reciprocal.

IV. Domestic and External Factors Affecting Cross-Strait Relations

International Factors

The various factors influencing relations between the two sides of the Taiwan Strait may be roughly divided into three categories: international factors, factors originating in = mainland China, and factors within Taiwan itself. As far as international factors are concerned, the international community may be said to have entered a new era in the 1990s. After an experiment lasting more than seventy years, communism proved itself to be ultimately unacceptable. This was because the communist countries had long used the "dictatorship of the proletariat" to suppress freedom and democracy, thus provoking dissatisfaction and resistance from all strata of society, while the system of socialist public ownership and the planned economy had resulted in economic stagnation, making it impossible to raise living standards. These were the chief reasons for the disintegration of the Soviet Union and the collapse of communism in Eastern Europe. In the post-Cold War situation, the PRC's role as a strategic ally of the West underwent a change; the Western countries began to pay more attention to the suppression of human rights in mainland China, and the international community began to take a more reasonable attitude toward the division of China under two separate governments on either side of the Taiwan Strait. Other countries also realized that the Republic of China could play a role in the mainland's reform and opening up process, and recognized the importance of security in the Taiwan Strait to the stability of Asia and the economic development of the Asia-Pacific region.

In addition, the growing importance of economic interdependence in international relations has also been beneficial to cross- detente. In 1991, Taiwan, mainland China, and Hong Kong all joined the Asia-Pacific Economic Cooperation (APEC) forum, and the two sides of the Strait are expected to be joining the General Agreement on Tariffs and Trade (GATT) in the near future. The increased prosperity that economic liberalization is bringing to the Asia-Pacific region will encourage Peking to speed up the pace of reform and opening up, which will benefit cross-Strait relations and narrow the gap between the two sides, thus creating conditions advantageous to the peaceful unification of China.

International trends toward integration and division are also having an impact on relations between the two sides of the Taiwan Strait. During the Cold War period when ideology was all-important, the unification policies of divided countries were usually influenced by bloc politics and as a result tended to be uncompromising. Unification was necessarily carried out by force. Since the end of the Cold War, the reemergence of the idea of integration has encouraged divided countries to start once again on the path to unification.

One example is the way that the East German people's desire for a free and democratic political and economic system and the national sentiments of the people of West Germany brought about the democratic unification of Germany in October 1990. Another example is how North and South Korea, on the basis of peace and parity, signed a non-aggression and reconciliation pact in December 1991. These examples of divided countries being encouraged to progress toward detente and unification by changes in the world political and economic order are characteristic of the post-Cold War period.

Also since the end of the Cold War, some long-repressed ethnic groups have experienced a revival of nationalism which has engendered notable separatist demands. The Soviet Union, for example, has split into fifteen separate countries, while the two ethnic groups making up Czechoslovakia agreed by common consent to divide into two separate states: the Czech Republic and Slovakia. Yugoslavia was also influenced by separatism and has disintegrated as a result.

These two trends of integration and separatism have had an impact on Taiwan too. In Taiwan, the passing of the "Guidelines for National Unification" was an affirmation of the trend toward integration, while on the other hand, proposals for Taiwan independence have been stimulated by the separatist trend. The ROC government believes that the unification of China is the common aspiration of Chinese people at home and abroad in their quest for a strong and prosperous country and the long-term development of the Chinese nation. We want to encourage the realization of this goal. However, we have to admit that Taiwan is a democratic society, with complete freedom of speech and thought, which has inevitably been influenced by both integration and separatist ideas. Subjectively speaking, the ROC government believes that we should work toward integration, but in objective terms, the degree of acceptance which these two trends enjoy among the people of Taiwan will depend on the future development of relations between the two sides of the Taiwan Strait. If cross-Strait relations do not develop favorably, the shadow of separatism is not likely to be dispelled and may indeed grow darker still in Taiwan. On the other hand, if there is friendly interaction between the two sides, the development of separatism will be hindered.

Factors within Mainland China

The situation within mainland China and the CCP regime's policy toward Taiwan constitute another set of factors influencing cross-Strait relations. The goal of the Republic of China's mainland policy is to establish a political and economic system and a way of life conducive to the survival and development of the entire Chinese people. We are pleased that Peking has speeded up the pace of its economic reform and opening up. However, we also notice that although the Peking authorities have decided to establish a "Chinese-style socialist market economy" to promote economic development and improve the people's standard of living, and also to serve as a basis for the continuation of their regime, politically they are still upholding the so-called "four cardinal principles" (the socialist road, the people's democratic dictatorship, the leadership of the Communist Party, and Marxism-Leninism-Mao Tse-tung thought) which underpin their one-party dictatorship. This policy of political "leftism" and economic "rightism" is riddled with inconsistencies. The unending economic and financial crises that mainland China has suffered in recent years, the widening gap between rich and poor, and the appearance of all kinds of social problems are all results of this policy. If the Chinese Communists do not undertake political reforms hey will find it difficult to break out of the economic vicious circle they have been trapped in for so long, with its periodic loosening and tightening of restrictions. Domestic political trends in mainland China will have an impact on the Taiwan people's attitude to unification. Whenever the Taiwan people are asked in public opinion polls whether they prefer unification or Taiwan independence, a far higher proportion opt for the former rather than the latter when the condition is that mainland China is a liberal democracy. In contrast, when the condition is that Peking remains a one-party dictatorship, the proportion of respondents who prefer unification falls abruptly, while support for independence rises. From this it is obvious that the degree of democracy or dictatorship on the mainland will have a deep impact on the Taiwan people's views on unification.

Peking's Taiwan policy also has an impact on the Taiwan public's feelings about unification. The CCP leaders have never relinquished the threat of using force against Taiwan. In addition, Peking has always sought to prevent the Republic of China from participating in international activities and tried to have it removed from various international organizations or its status downgraded. Peking has also done its utmost to sabotage the Republic of China's relations with its friends, hindering it from developing aviation rights, purchasing arms and military equipment necessary for its defense, and exchanging high-level official visits and developing normal contacts with other countries. Hostile actions such as these naturally make Chinese people in Taiwan wonder why their own brethren should seek to harm them.

The Chinese Communists have enforced this diplomatic blockade for many years, seemingly without realizing that it contains the following inconsistencies. Firstly, Peking is making use of international forces to besiege Taiwan, while at the same time opposing the "internationalization" of the so-called Taiwan question; secondly, it claims that when Taiwan opens air links with foreign countries this is a "political issue with an impact on sovereignty," while at the same time claiming that the question of direct flights between Taiwan and the mainland is purely an economic issue; and thirdly, it is trying to restrict the international activities of the people of Taiwan, Penghu, Kinmen and Matsu, on which their prosperity depends, while simultaneously harping on about "national sentiment." If Peking does not wake up to the fact that its actions do not correspond to its words, and if it continues to use high-pressure tactics to elbow the Republic of China out of the international community, it will not only fail in its task, it may also stir up more hatred for its regime in Taiwan and obstruct progress toward national unification.

To tell the truth, in some areas of international relations the interests of the two sides of the Taiwan Strait already run parallel to each other. It is a pity that the Chinese Communists have not taken this into consideration and have instead allowed the two sides to waste their precious resources and energies on a diplomatic struggle. If the two sides could only coexist in the international community, both would have more room to maneuver on the world stage; the Chinese people would have a louder voice in international affairs and would no longer cancel each other out. Not only that, this multifaceted learning process would be conducive to reasonable contacts between the two sides, foster brotherly feeling between them, and increase the likelihood of eventual unification. As for the Republic of China's bid to join the United Nations, if we could successfully participate in all UN organizations and activities and use the experiences accumulated over the past four decades or more to make a contribution to the international community, winning even more international respect for the Chinese people, the CCP regime would have no reason for trying to stop us, as long as this was done on condition that the two sides of the Strait declare publicly that they are seeking a united China. The experience of East and West Germany shows us that joint participation by the two halves of a divided nation in the international community by no means damages the prospects for unification--indeed, it can have the effect of easing tension and creating conditions favorable to unification as well as safeguarding the interests of the entire people. Not so long ago, North and South Korea adopted a similar course of action. We believe that in this era of detente, the two sides of the Taiwan Strait should think of some way to dispel their hostility. The ROC government has already taken a big step forward in this direction, and if Peking can understand this and make a response, we are confident that this will facilitate the development of cross-Strait relations toward unification.

Factors Arising from Developments within Taiwan

Another factor influencing relations between the two sides of the Taiwan Strait is the future political and economic development of Taiwan. It might be said that the Republic of China on Taiwan has undergone a quiet revolution in recent years. Economically, it has become the world's fourteenth largest trading nation, and the world's seventh largest foreign investor. It is also ranked twentieth in the world in terms of average per capita income, and the government's foreign exchange reserves are almost without equal. Politically speaking, the Republic of China has established the first democracy in China's history, according respect for human rights and the rule of law. After this accumulation of economic strength and social and cultural vitality had found its release through democratization and liberalization, it had an impact in two directions: toward the outside world in the shape of the ROC's "pragmatic diplomacy," and toward mainland China where it has acted as an important catalyst for the expansion of all kinds of people-to-people exchanges. Thus, recent developments in cross-Strait relations may be seen as originating to a large extent in Taiwan's economic growth and political democratization.

It is a pity that the Peking authorities have not only failed to understand this cause and effect relationship, but actually ridicule or attack Taiwan's democratization process, and accuse us of pursuing a "two Chinas" or "one China, one Taiwan" policy in the name of pragmatic diplomacy. They unreasonably interfere with the Republic of China's external relations and scheme to reduce the scope of its international activities. At the same time, Peking is attempting to "use trade and investment for political ends and to use the people to pressure the government" in an effort to expand its influence over Taiwan and force the ROC government to accept its "one country, two systems" arrangement. This combination of persuasion and pressure fails to take into account political and economic development trends in Taiwan in recent years and pays no regard whatsoever to the real wishes and welfare of the people of Taiwan. If it continues, it will inevitably have a negative impact on the unification of China and normal exchanges between the two sides of the Strait.

Since the lifting of martial law and the ban on the formation of new political parties in 1987, the rights of assembly and association and freedom of speech granted by the Constitution have been completely guaranteed in Taiwan. A consensus has gradually been formed among the people of Taiwan that we are "all in the same boat" and that Taiwan is *agemeinschaft*, or community. This belief in a Taiwan community does not by any means imply that Taiwan's 21 million people are indifferent to Chinese history or that they have abandoned the ideal of a unified China,it simply means that their future welfare and security are closely bound up with the fate of Taiwan. Another manifestation of this feeling of community is the way in which public opinion plays a guiding role in government policy-making. In the course of formulating its mainland policy, the ROC government must periodically consult a wide range of public opinion. As democracy matures in Taiwan, public opinion will necessarily become the government's most important reference for formulating mainland policy.

Taiwan is already a democratic, pluralistic society. Opposition members occupy a considerable number of seats in the Legislative Yuan, and their opinions inevitably have an influence on the government's mainland policy. Where national identity and cross-Strait relations are concerned, the ruling party and the opposition differ quite considerably. But although the various parties may have different opinions concerning mainland policy, their ultimate purpose is to consider the welfare of the people of Taiwan. They always have to give careful consideration as to the impact of their proposals on the security and welfare of Taiwan's 21 million people. Furthermore, what the ROC government and the Peking authorities should be struggling for is the long-term well-being of the entire Chinese people. In this struggle, any rash proposals or distortions of national identity will go against the interests of all Chinese people.

V. Conclusion

Division Is a Misfortune for the Chinese People

The division of China under two separate governments is a great misfortune for the Chinese people, less so for the Chinese people on Taiwan. After the communist takeover of mainland China, the territory of Taiwan, Penghu, Kinmen, and Matsu was preserved as a base for nurturing China's future vitality. After forty years of effort, the Republic of China on Taiwan has created a degree of democracy and prosperity unprecedented in Chinese history. These forty years or more have seen the transformation of Taiwan from a remote offshore island into a pivotal force directing China's future.

The government of the Republic of China led the Chinese people through eight years of bloody war to a final victory over the Japanese imperialist invaders, abrogated the unequal treaties, and made China a founding member of the United Nations with a permanent seat on its Security Council. But since the Peking regime was established in mainland China in 1949, the people of the mainland have suffered. The CCP regime has endlessly provoked military clashes with its neighbors, while at home it has been racked by power struggles and purges, creating a situation of backwardness and destitution under communist rule.

The Contribution Peking Should Make Toward Unification

We call on the CCP to further promote its economic reforms and carry out all-round political reform, as this alone can deliver our mainland compatriots from poverty and want and allow them to live lives of humanity and dignity. We also call on the Peking regime to face up to the problems confronting relations between the two sides of the Taiwan Strait, to realize the fact that China is a divided country under two separate governments, and to pursue the development of cross-Strait relations in earnest according to the principles of reason, peace, parity, and reciprocity. This is the only way we can create an opportunity for the peaceful unification of China.

We believe that the Chinese people are absolutely opposed to either military threats or the devastation of war. Threats only increase mutual hostility and war would destroy both sides. Anyone who resorts to arms in the name of unification will be condemned by history. Only when we develop our fellow feeling as Chinese and treat each other equally will the obstacles to cross-Strait relations be overcome and will we draw closer together.

The True Worth of Unification Lies in Democracy, Freedom, and Equitable Prosperity

"Peaceful unification," however, is not enough; we should have "democratic unification." Only unification under a free and democratic system will give the Chinese people happiness and enable China to make a greater contribution to world peace, security, and prosperity. If China were unified under a dictatorship and human rights were violated, it would pose a grave threat to world peace and as such would not be tolerated by other countries. At the same time, we believe that the real significance of unification lies not only in the achievement of a strong and prosperous country and the long-term development of the Chinese nation, it also lies in enabling the Chinese people to enjoy democracy, freedom, and equitable prosperity. If we cannot achieve this, unification will be completely meaningless and worthless.

Looking back over the past and forward to the future, the ROC government will continue to adhere to the stance of "giving priority to humanitarian concerns and gradually expanding people-to-people exchanges, increasing mutual understanding by focussing on cultural exchange, and expanding economic and trade ties according to the principles of complementarily and mutual benefit." We will make every effort to promote cross-Strait relations to encourage the favorable development of interaction between the two sides. The ROC government will also continue to devise a forward-looking, pragmatic, active, and moderate strategy for overall exchanges, and will neither draw back on account of Peking's hostility, nor make rash advances in response to Peking's enticements. We are confident that the wisdom and efforts of the entire Chinese people will help us to create a new situation, speed up political, economic, and social modernization in mainland China, and eventually complete the sacred mission of unifying China under democracy, freedom, and equitable prosperity.

Guidelines for National Unification

Adopted by the National Unification Council at its third meeting on February 23, 1991, and by the Executive Yuan Council (Cabinet) at its 2223rd meeting on March 14, 1991.

I. Forward

The unification of China is meant to bring about a strong and prosperous nation with a long-lasting, bright future for its people; it is the common wish of the Chinese people at home and aborad. After an appropriate period of forthright exchange, cooperation, and consultation conducted under the principles of reason, peace, parity, and reciprocity, the two sides of the Taiwan Straits should foster a consensus of democracy, freedom and equal prosperity, and together build anew a unified China. Based on this understanding, these Guidelines have been specially formulated with the express hope that all Chinese throughout the world will work with one mind toward their fulfillment.

II. Goal

To establish a democratic, free and equitably prosperous China.

III. Principles

(1) Both the mainland and Taiwan areas are parts of Chinese territory. Helping to bring about national unification should be the common responsibility of all the Chinese people.

(2) The unification of China should be for the welfare of all its people and not be subject to partisan conflict.

(3) China's unification should aim at promoting Chinese culture, safeguarding human dignity, guaranteeing fundamental mental human rights, and practicing democracy and the rule of law.

(4) The timing and manner of China's unification should first respect the rights and interests of the people in the Taiwan area, and protect

their security and welfare.   It should be achieved in gradual phases under the principles of reason, peace, parity, and reciprocity.

IV. Process

1. Short term —a phase of exchanges and reciprocity.

(1) To enhance understanding through exchanges between the two sides of the Straits and eliminate hostility through reciprocity; and to establish a mutually benign relationship by not endangering each other's security and stability while in the midst of exchanges ad not denying the other's existence as a political entity while in the midst of effecting reciprocity.

(2) To set up an order for exchanges across the Straits, to draw up regulations for such exchanges, and to establish intermediary organizations so as to protect people's rights and interests on both sides of the Straits; to gradually ease various restrictions and expand people-to people contacts so as to promote the social prosperity of both sides.

(3) In order to improve the people's welfare on both sides of the Straits with the ultimate objective of unifying the nation, in the mainland area economic reform should be carried out forthrightly, the expression of public opinion there should gradually be allowed, and both democracy and the rule of law should be implemented; while the in Taiwan area efforts should be made to accelerate constitutional reform and promote national development to establish a society of equitable prosperity.

(4) The two sides of the Straits should end the state of hostility and, under the principle of one China, solve all disputes through peaceful means, and furthermore respect--not reject--each other in the international community, so as to move toward a phase of mutual trust and cooperation.

2. Medium Term--a phase of mutual trust and cooperation.

(1) Both sides of the Straits should establish official communication channels on equal footing.

(2) Direct postal, transport and commercial links should be allowed, and both sides should jointly develop the southeastern coastal area of the Chinese mainland and then gradually extend this development to other areas of the mainland in order to narrow the gap in living standards between the two sides.

(3) Both sides of the Straits should work together and assist each other in taking part in international organizations and activities.

(4) Mutual visits by high-ranking officials on both sides should be promoted to create favorable conditions for consultation and unification.

3. Long term--a phase of consultation and unification

A consultative organization for unification should be established through which both sides, in accordance with the will of the people in both the mainland and Taiwan areas, and while adhering to the goals of democracy, economic freedom, social justice and nationalization of the armed forces, jointly discuss the grand task of unification and map out a constitutional system to establish a democratic, free and equitable prosperous China.

About the Author

John F. Copper is the Stanley J. Buckman Distinguished Professor of International Studies at Rhodes College in Memphis, Tennessee. He is the author of sixteen books on Chinese and Asian affairs. His book *China's Global Role* (1980) won the Clarence Day Foundation Award for outstanding research and creativity. Professor Copper's most recent books are: *Taiwan: Nation-State or Province?* (1990),*China Diplomacy:The Washington-Taipei-Beijing Triangle* (1992), *Historical Dictionary of Taiwan* (1993) and *Taiwan's 1991 and 1992 Non-Supplemental Elections: Reaching a Higher State of Democracy* (1994).

Dr. Copper is also the author of numerous articles and opinion pieces. He has lived in Asia for thirteen years.